MITCHELL BEAZLEY
DISCOVERING WINE COUNTRY

Burgundy

Patrick Matthews

For Stella Pe-Win

DISCOVERING WINE COUNTRY
BURGUNDY
by Patrick Matthews

First published in Great Britain in 2005
by Mitchell Beazley, an imprint of Octopus Publishing Group Limited,
2–4 Heron Quays, London E14 4JP.

A CIP catalogue record for this book is available from the British Library.

ISBN: 1 84533 036 6

The author and publishers will be grateful for any information which will assist them in keeping future editions up-to-date. Although all reasonable care has been taken in the preparation of this book, neither the publishers nor the author can accept any liability for any consequences arising from the use thereof, or the information contained therein.

Photographs by Victoria McTernan
Map creation by Encompass Graphics

Commissioning Editor Hilary Lumsden
Executive Art Editor Yasia Williams-Leedham
Senior Designer Tim Pattinson
Managing Editor Julie Sheppard
Editor Margaret Rand
Designer Gaelle Lochner
Index Hilary Bird
Production Gary Hayes

Typeset in Futura and Sabon

Printed and bound by Toppan Printing Company in China

ACKNOWLEDGEMENTS

In addition to everyone involved in the project, I would especially like to thank Hilary Lumsden for backing the idea, and also, in France, to Lucien Antoni, Vincent Bruno, Harry Coen, Sally Duerdoth, Anne Mathon, Susan Matthews, Matthew Meadows, David Thornton and Becky Wasserman for helping me learn more about Burgundy and Beaujolais.

Thanks to Editions JYP Repro of Le Creusot for permission to reproduce the material in the box on p.13. And the publishers would like to thank Eurotunnel plc for their assistance with my travel arrangements.

Contents

How to use this book

Discovering Wine Country is all about getting you from the page to the producer. Each chapter covers a specific winemaking region of interest, and includes a map of the area featured, with places of interest marked using the symbols below. The leading wine producers mentioned are all given a map grid reference so you can see exactly where they are.

The maps include key features to help you navigate your way round the routes, but they are not intended to replace detailed road maps, or indeed detailed vineyard maps, normally available from local tourist offices or the local wine bureau (*see* below right).

It wouldn't be practical to mark each and every grower on the maps. Instead the sign ❧ means that an area or village is home to at least one recommended wine producer. The wine regions covered are packed with other points of interest for the wine enthusiast but that are unrelated to actual wine purchasing. These are shown as ⛪ Sometimes this includes growers who don't sell direct but whose status is such that they will be on any wine-lover's itinerary. Exceptional restaurants are marked ℀ and towns and villages where there's an Office de Tourism are marked ⓘ which is especially useful for finding *gîtes* and campsites.

Quick reference map symbols
❧ recommended wine producer
⛪ wine tourist site
★ tourist attraction
℀ recommended restaurant
ⓘ tourist information centre

▬▬▬ named wine region

 author's suggested wine route(s) to follow, with information about how long the route is and any other useful tips.

│ Voie Verte cycle route

 scale bar

Ⓝ north compass

Boxed information
the contact details of hotels, restaurants, tourist information, hire shops, transport facilities, and other points of interest.

wine-related information as well as the author's selection of the top growers to visit in the specific area featured, including contact details, a map reference, and a price indicator:
inexpensive: <€6.50
moderate: €6.50–10
expensive: €10–20

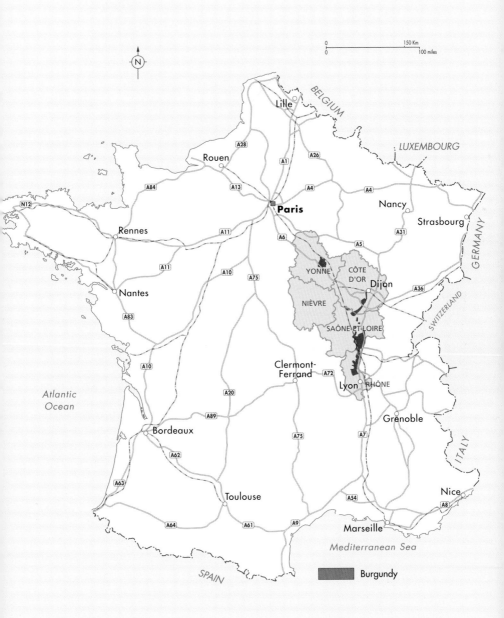

0   150 Km
0   100 miles

N

BELGIUM

LUXEMBOURG

Lille

A28

Rouen

A1

A26

A84

A13

A4

A4

Nancy

Strasbourg

GERMANY

N12

Paris

A6

A11

A5

A31

Rennes

A36

A11

YONNE

CÔTE
D'OR

Dijon

SWITZERLAND

A10

A75

NIÈVRE

Nantes

A83

SAÔNE-ET-LOIRE

Atlantic
Ocean

A10

Clermont-
Ferrand

A72

Lyon

RHÔNE

A20

Grenoble

A89

Bordeaux

A75

A7

ITALY

A62

A63

Nice

Toulouse

A54

A8

A64

A61

A9

Marseille

SPAIN

Mediterranean Sea

Burgundy

Local wine bureau

BIVB (Bureau Interprofessionnel
des Vins du Bourgone),
www.vins-bourgogne.fr

Introduction

When I'm on holiday, I find I need a mission – otherwise all that leisure can become as draining as uninterrupted work – and this book describes the perfect one. If you like wine, and enjoy being in France, you owe it to yourself to visit some growers and buy from them direct. You will meet interesting people, visit beautiful places, learn how wine is made, and should also save quite a bit of money. You will also end up with much more varied and interesting wine than you can find even from an enterprising importer, let alone your local supermarket.

ABOVE *Pile 'em high: the French are addicted to buying directly, as here at the cooperative in Buxy .*

A sight for sore eyes

When you drive up to a small property in Burgundy you aren't a tourist, but that most welcome sight, a potential *client particulier*, or private customer. I hope this book will help make the experience go smoothly, by offering a shortlist of good producers, giving you some background information on the villages, their wines and their local history, and – most important, yet sometimes most challenging – stopping you from getting lost.

Cellar door sales are an important business in most of the world's wine regions. But Burgundy is unique, because the landholdings are so small (in all there are around 7,800 different growers, if you include Beaujolais). Instead of going to a visitor centre, you will almost certainly find yourself tasting with the man or woman who planted the vines, pruned them, ploughed the land, oversaw the harvesting, and made the wine – sometimes sleeping beside the vats to keep an eye on the fermentation.

The Burgundian approach

Burgundy is where I first learned about wine. There could be no better place to start. When you go to other wine areas, you realize that Burgundy is not just a region, but a shorthand for a whole approach to wine.

In Bordeaux, the most expensive, and fashionable, producers have now adopted the techniques practised by generations of Burgundian peasants. In California and Australia as well, invariably it's the most creative and sensitive winemakers who show the greatest interest in Burgundy, its grapes, its soils and its traditions.

You could sum up the Burgundian philosophy as: respect for nature, hands-on winemaking (being guided by the senses of taste, smell, touch and sight rather than lab reports), and a humility about the role of the winemaker.

Affordability and availability
I wanted to write this book because I was astonished to find that so many lovely wines were a) affordable, and b) unavailable except from the growers. The two things are linked, in fact. The international wine trade likes to deal in stuff that's very cheap to produce — so that there's room to make a profit — or expensive, so that their margins appear as only a small proportion of the total selling price.

If you buy directly from the growers, both parties in the transaction benefit. Producers get only a small fraction of the shelf price of a wine sold abroad — if they sell to Great Britain, for example, they often receive far less than is pocketed by the government in taxes and the retailer in profits.

But if you pay even as little as €4.50 to a conscientious grower, he or she will, literally, plough back the profits. I am always amazed that Burgundian farmers use techniques that their Californian equivalents would think uneconomical for wines selling for twice or three times the price.

Take the president of the producers' association of the Côtes du Couchois, Bernard Royet. No one I know in Britain has even heard of the Côtes du Couchois — although these vineyards, created by the bishops of Autun, are some of the oldest in Burgundy. When Royet sells his red wine to a shipper, he gets less than €2 a bottle. Yet he and his son Jean-Claude make the wine as if it was from a world-famous village like Puligny or Pommard. Why, I asked him, when this makes no business sense? "There's no law against it, is there?" he replied.

But what if the wine turns out to be rubbish?
The main argument against buying direct is that you'll end up with something undrinkable. It's true that you may encounter the odd wine tainted by a faulty cork. If so you can always ask for a replacement on a subsequent visit.

Otherwise, you are the best judge of what you like. You may later wish you'd bought more of one thing and less of another — but that is how you learn and acquire the only kind of expertise that matters.

Don't spend all your money, though, on ultra-expensive *grands crus*. An importer will know better how these will mature. This book is about more everyday stuff. And spread your options: if you buy from a number of sources you will make more discoveries and minimize any disappointments.

IN THE FOOTSTEPS OF FRANK SCHOONMAKER, 1905–76

In an ancient wine region like Burgundy it's easy to imagine that things have always been done the same way. But when you **follow one of the many signs in a village to find a family of growers who bottle and sell their own wine,** you're following in the footsteps of an extraordinary American: a journalist, wine importer and spy called **Frank Schoonmaker**.

Schoonmaker was a young travel journalist and author of such books as *Through Europe on $2 a Day* in the late 1920s. One day he treated himself to **lunch at one of Paris's top restaurants, Le Roy Gourmet**, in the seventeenth-century Place des Victoires. A waiter introduced him to a regular customer, **Raymond Baudouin**, who edited France's first specialist consumer wine magazine, *La Revue du Vin de France*.

Baudouin was **encouraging growers to bottle their wine themselves** rather than sell through merchants, who were notorious for inauthentic and misleading labelling. **Schoonmaker learned about wine from the Frenchman** and accompanied him around the vineyards. When Prohibition ended in 1933 **Schoonmaker went into business as a wine importer.**

The idea of selling growers' wines overseas was not Schoonmaker's only legacy. He **first came up with the idea** of selling Californian wines, not under names such as "Burgundy" and "Chablis" to which they clearly weren't entitled, but as **"Cabernet" or "Chardonnay", after the** name of the grape variety.

Understanding
Burgundy

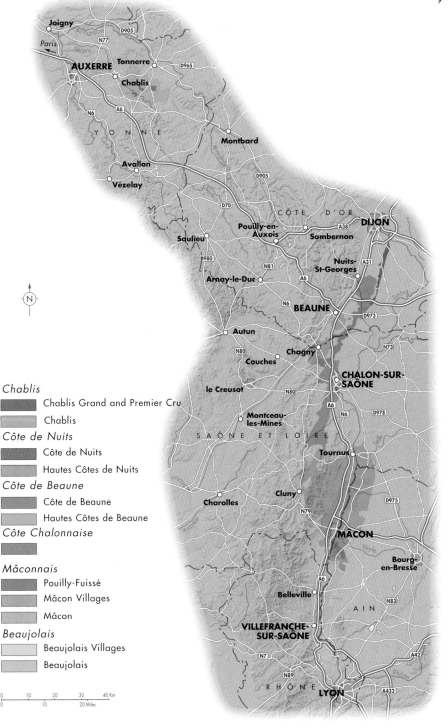

Chablis

- Chablis Grand and Premier Cru
- Chablis

Côte de Nuits

- Côte de Nuits
- Hautes Côtes de Nuits

Côte de Beaune

- Côte de Beaune
- Hautes Côtes de Beaune

Côte Chalonnaise

Mâconnais

- Pouilly-Fuissé
- Mâcon Villages
- Mâcon

Beaujolais

- Beaujolais Villages
- Beaujolais

| 0 | 10 | 20 | 30 | 40 Km |
| 0 | | 10 | | 20 Miles |

Joigny
Paris
N77
D905
AUXERRE
Tonnerre
Chablis
D965
N6
A6
Y O N N E
Montbard
Avallon
Vézelay
D905
D70
C Ô T E   D ' O R
Pouilly-en-Auxois
A38
DIJON
Saulieu
Sombernon
D980
N81
Nuits-St-Georges
A31
Arnay-le-Duc
A6
N6
BEAUNE
D973
Autun
N73
Chagny
N80
Couches
CHALON-SUR-SAÔNE
le Creusot
N80
A6
N6
D978
Montceau-les-Mines
S A Ô N E   E T   L O I R E
Tournus
Cluny
D975
Charolles
N79
MÂCON
Bourg-en-Bresse
Veyle
A6
Belleville
N83
A I N
VILLEFRANCHE-SUR-SAÔNE
N7
A42
N89
Rhône
R H Ô N E
LYON
A432

Why Burgundy?

B urgundy has the most famous name of perhaps any wine region in the world apart from Champagne. And like Champagne, its name has been widely misused. In the English-speaking world "Burgundy" came (incorrectly) to mean any rich, red wine. "I started out on burgundy" (Bob Dylan, 1965) refers to all-American "hearty burgundy" from California, though Dylan was enthusiastic about genuine Beaujolais in the mid-1960s.

ABOVE *Invented tradition. These wine-growers' "medieval" robes were designed as recently as the 1940s.*

RIGHT *Timeless. The polychromatic roof tiles fashionable in the late middle ages now help give Burgundy its visual identity.*

European rules

These days, unless you're American, a wine called "burgundy" really has to come from Burgundy. But there's still a question of definition. The French revolution abolished the province when it subdivided France into a number of smaller *départements*. Burgundy was not reborn until 1982 and the creation of the "Région Bourgogne", which includes the *départements* of Côte d'Or, Nièvre, Saône-et-Loire, and Yonne. But administrative Burgundy is not the same as wine burgundy. Nièvre, for example, makes a world-famous wine, Pouilly-Fumé (not to be confused with Pouilly-Fuissé from Saône-et-Loire); but this is classed as a Loire wine, not a burgundy.

Beaujolais – part of Burgundy?

Then there's Beaujolais. The two most northerly Beaujolais villages (St-Amour and Juliénas) are in Saône-et-Loire and not, like the others, in the *département* of Rhône. Let's be clear: Beaujolais isn't Burgundy. It's a region with a different history, traditions, and a different look. Beaujolais arguably deserves its own guide. It's a region of great beauty and there are some terrific wine bargains to be had – particularly as it's fallen from fashion in many of its former markets. For our readers' convenience, if not for reasons of logic, it is included here, from p.121 onwards.

Is burgundy worth all the fuss?

Burgundy has been planted with vines since Roman times, but wine-growing was developed by Benedictine and Cistercian monks in the middle ages. At this time the local market for wines was Dijon, the capital of the independent duchy of Burgundy. But by the eighteenth century the English writer Henry Fielding could describe burgundy as the most sought-after French wine.

Many French people would say that the southeast-facing slopes of the Côte d'Or, with their clay and limestone soils, are simply the best places in the world to grow grapes to make red wine from Pinot Noir and white from Chardonnay. If you want to buy directly from the growers, you also have the pleasure of visiting a beautiful region, free from modern intensive farming, studded with fascinating old churches and châteaux, and food that is some of the best in France.

Too much choice?

No two burgundies are quite the same; the different patches of land give different results, and so do the hundreds of individual winemakers. This diversity can be a nightmare in selling to a world that's used to recognizable brand names. But the marketing woes of Burgundy's growers can give rise to some extraordinary bargains – especially from the little-known and out-of-the way villages listed in this book.

But for some, there's a catch. Robert Parker, a top US wine critic, believes that while the most expensive wines may be beyond reproach, cheaper burgundies aren't worth bothering with. It depends, though, on what you're used to. For several decades now, wines all round the world have been made to taste more like sun-baked Californian wines, with less emphasis on the delicate red-fruit flavours of red burgundy. These flavours may be an acquired taste, but once hooked, you'll find yourself searching for them elsewhere – and usually looking in vain.

The Burgundians

B urgundy is a big place. It has no obvious geographical boundaries; it covers a larger area than Belgium and it feels the pull of France's two largest cities: Paris to the north and Lyon to the south. One way to think of Burgundy is in terms of transit and communication, linking northern Europe with the Mediterranean. Seen this way, the key features of Burgundy aren't mountains or forests, but man-made links: the canal system, built in the seventeenth century, the nineteenth-century railway, and more recently motorways such as the Paris-Lyon A6, and the TGV, the high-speed train that skirts the vineyards of Chablis and hurtles through the heart of the Mâconnais.

Iron and steel, food, and wine

It's more than a wine region. The iron and steel region around the TGV station of Le Creusot-Monchanin-Monceau-les-Mines powered France's industrial revolution, and Le Creusot, west of Chalon-Sur-Saône, is still the main manufacturing centre for high-speed trains. Visitors to this town are greeted by a vast 1875-vintage precision steam hammer, whose thudding once carried for a distance of more than 10km (6 miles).

RIGHT They really do eat frogs here, and the restaurants aren't shy of advertising this.

BELOW A giant steam-hammer dating from 1875; a relic of Burgundy's heavy industry.

Burgundy is also a big food producer – famous for its Dijon mustard (mixed with sour grape juice, or *verjus*), its soft fruit, its cream-coloured Charolais cattle, and its free-range chickens: Poulets de Bresse are the only fowl in the world to be certified, like wine, by an *appellation contrôlée* system that guarantees their origin and the way they've been reared.

But the vineyards are the chief symbol of Burgundy's identity. This is partly because of where they are: the Côte d'Or begins in the outskirts of Burgundy's capital, Dijon, the seat of the medieval dukes of Burgundy, whose territories in the late middle ages stretched as far as what are now Holland, Luxembourg and the Jura. (They didn't however include Beaujolais. This was a separate duchy, ruled for five centuries by the sires or lords of Beaujeu, from their château of Pierre-Aigüe.)

The role of the monks

The vineyards are the legacy of Burgundy's other great gift to the world – the development of western monasticism. The famous "Rule", or instructions of St Benedict, dates from sixth-century Italy, but the Benedictine order took on a distinctive character following the reforms put in place at the great monastery founded at Cluny (*see* p.112) in AD910. The other

great order, that of the white-robed Cistercians, was founded less than a century later, and took its name from the new monastery of Cîteaux, 14.5km (9 miles) from Nuits-St-Georges. The Cistercians, or rather the lay brothers responsible for farm work, mapped out the great walled vineyards of the Côte d'Or.

With the dissolution of the monasteries after the Revolution the state sold off the vineyards to local smallholders, and these little estates, with holdings split between different villages, are distinctively Burgundian.

To Parisians, Burgundian winemakers are peasants *par excellence*, offering *La France profonde* (a phrase that carries the idea of "the depths of the countryside") that's nonetheless conveniently accessible via the A6 motorway. The older generation of Burgundians speaks with a strong accent, rolling the Rs and elongating the vowels: a place-name like Les Hautes-Côtes de Beaune can take forever and a day to pronounce in the mouth of an-aged *vigneron*, or wine-grower.

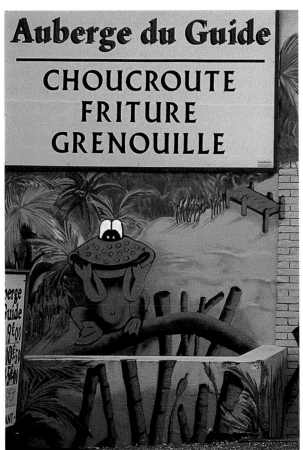

**HOW TO TALK BURGUNDIAN
(SOME INESSENTIAL PHRASES)**

The sound of Burgundian French is a kind of gentle mooing (perhaps learned from proximity to the Charolais cattle), achieved partly by lengthening some vowels, and doing away with the shorter ones.

So, if you're asking a *vigneron* if he could give you a tasting you might politely add:
"Si t'ai du temps d'reste."
("If you're not too busy.")

If it's a wet day, you could observe that:
"Yen rouche comme vache qui pisse."
("It's raining cats and dogs.")

The poor weather might have adverse consequences for the young vines, so you could follow on with:
"Les pessiaûx c't'année y sont toûss' peûrtillés."
("The vine shoots are all wormy this year.")

Faced with these misfortunes, it might be well to sympathize with your *vigneron*:
"Qu'aî qu't'aî don? Te v'la t'us blanc qu'une patte."
("Are you sure you're all right? You seem a little pale.")

If your eloquence in the dialect surprises the farmer, he might in turn respond that:
"T'ai b'en d'la joue c'matin."
("You are very talkative this morning.")

(SOURCE: Lucien Gauthe, Le Causer du Creusot, Editions JYB Repro.)

Seasons and festivals

There's really no bad time to go to Burgundy – but the experience can vary greatly according to the season. One of the best times to visit growers is in October, when the grape harvest is over and the vine leaves blaze brilliantly yellow along the whole 56km (35-mile) ribbon of vineyards, from Dijon down to Chagny. Autumn is also a good time to buy. It's when some of the most sought-after wines are briefly available in the first three months after they've been bottled, having spent a year in barrel. And the cooler weather means there's no risk of ruining your bottles by letting them bake in the back of an overheated car on the return journey through France.

RIGHT *Mâcon has a long-established wine fair, held each spring.*

BELOW *The end of the grape harvest is the cue for traditional festivities – and for some more informal ones.*

Three days of eating

A month after the clocks go back there is the most famous of all Burgundy's wine festivals: the Trois Glorieuses: three glorious days of formal banqueting, for those with an invitation and a taste for this kind of thing. The days are the Saturday, Sunday, and Monday of the third weekend in November, and centre around Sunday's charity auction of newly made wines from the vineyards owned by Beaune's fifteenth-century hospital foundation, the Hospices de Beaune. Wine professionals find that the prices achieved are a marker of the strength of the market in Burgundy, and of interest in fine French wine generally. They don't, however, reflect normal retail prices. There are also street celebrations and a giant tasting in the Palais des Congrès – the local convention centre. Chablis has its own Palais des Congrès and it holds its own Fête des Vins there the following weekend, the last in November.

Rituals by torchlight

At around the same time – the third Wednesday in November – there's the celebration of the release of Beaujolais Nouveau in Beaujeu – the ancient town that gave the region its name – with a procession lit by torches of blazing vine-shoots, or *sarmentelles*. In some countries Beaujolais Nouveau is fashionable, in others not, but in any case this is an interesting way to preview the wine.

Winter chill

Burgundy is almost as far as you can get in France from the moderating influence of the sea, and its continental climate can be bitterly cold in winter. But, December has an austere beauty.

In January the growers hold the most famous, or perhaps notorious, of wine celebrations: the St-Vincent, on the fourth Saturday of the month. Since 1938, except during the war and immediately afterwards, a different village each year has hosted it, with a procession, a Mass in honour of the patron saint of wine and of course a banquet.

What's special about the St-Vincent is the practice – under threat at the time of writing – of offering unlimited wine to

GRAPE-PICKING – PENANCE OR PARADISE?

Buying from a grower is one of **the best ways to learn about wine** – but it falls a good second to actually going out and **picking the grapes**.

This is very hard work: souvenirs of your fortnight are likely to include blisters, backache, and repetitive strain injury. You can also look forward to the frustration caused by your lack of knowledge of **French humour**, jokes and cursing, and probably to some ripe grape-bunches aimed to explode entertainingly on the back of your head.

On the other hand, it is likely to be **a life-changing event**. Many growers' wines are picked entirely by people who go back year after year for the experience – unpaid, but **fed and wined magnificently** by a back-up team often led by the grower's wife. Unless very privileged, you can expect to sleep semi-communally – at least sharing a room.

The best tip is to **choose a grower whose wines you admire** and which have some reputation – it's much more fun to be working among enthusiasts than in an anonymous crowd of students or itinerant farm-workers.

RIGHT *The top of the tree: there are no grander appellations than the Chambertin vineyard, or more respected names than Armand Rousseau.*

BELOW *Wine and its seasonal rituals give Burgundians a sense of place and of continuity with their winemaking ancestors.*

WINE FESTIVALS – DATES AND CONTACTS

All-Burgundy St-Vincent, fourth Saturday in January.

LOCAL ST-VINCENTS:
Auxerre (wines of the Yonne), third Sunday in January;
Mâconnais, week after main St-Vincent;
Chablis, the first full weekend in February.
Contact: BIVB
(Bureau Interprofessionel des Vins de Bourgogne)
Tel: 03 80 25 04 80
www.vins-bourgogne.fr

Nuits-St-Georges charity wine sale and all-Burgundy wine show, last weekend in March.
Contact: Nuits-St-Georges Town Hall
Tel: 03 80 62 01 35

Fête du Beaujolais Nouveau, Les Sarmentelles de Beaujeu, night of the third Wednesday in November.
Contact: Beaujeu Tourist Office, Tel: 04 74 69 22 88

Les Trois Glorieuses, third weekend in November. Main sale is 3pm Sunday. Dancing in streets of Beaune, wine show in Beaune's Palais des Congrès.
Contact: BIVB (see above).

all-comers. Tens of thousands regularly take up the offer, arriving not just from throughout France but from all over the world. It's a tribute to French drinking culture (see p.23) that though they get the worse for wear, there's rarely any violent disorder.

Flowers and Grands Jours

Spring is Burgundy is dramatic. The unsprayed fields become thickly strewn with cowslips, and the woods erupt with white blossom. Late March also sees Nuits-St-Georges' equivalent of Beaune's charity auction – Nuits has its own hospital foundation – and around ten thousand wine professionals descend on the region for the mammoth tasting called the Grands Jours de Bourgogne. Soon afterwards – on the first Sunday after Easter, one of the ten villages that make the top Beaujolais celebrates the Fête des Crus, with a tasting of the more distinguished wines that, unlike those that were sold as Nouveau in November, are said to have "celebrated Easter".

The flower of early summer is the blue iris. In both Burgundy and Beaujolais people take the trouble needed to keep patches of rhizomes weed-free. They bloom around the same time as the vines – which flower 100 days before the grape harvest.

Knowing the wines

Modern consumers expect and appreciate a huge range of choice, and variety is something Burgundy offers in dizzying abundance. The wine is made by thousands of different growers, and in most wine villages there will be a number of wines from each vineyard. Almost everyone in Burgundy is fascinated to observe the marked differences that a differently facing slope, or differently draining soil or type of soil can create in the finished wine. Then again, different grape varieties produce quite different results. Burgundy is sometimes thought of as home to two famous varieties: Pinot Noir for red wines and Chardonnay for whites. But that's far from being the full picture.

How to read wine labels

It's easy to understand Burgundy's wine labels if you think of a pyramid. At its base is the great majority of the wine, which is simply sold as red or white burgundy, "Appellation d'Origine Contrôlée (or AOC/AC for short) Bourgogne". This will almost certainly be from Pinot Noir (if red) or Chardonnay (if white) – but see the section on the Gamay grape, below. This is what's called the "regional" appellation. Next up in the

hierarchy are wines from a more tightly defined area – a village, for example Meursault, or a sub-region, like the Hautes-Côtes (upper slopes) above Beaune or Nuits-St-Georges.

Single-vineyard wines can be labelled *premier cru*, or "First Growth", in which case they will also carry the name of the local village (as in Beaune Clos des Mouches). At the top of the pyramid is the tiny amount of wine from *grand cru* ("Great Growth") vineyards (like Le Montrachet or Le Chambertin), which have their own ACs and travel without their village names.

Labels in Beaujolais

Beaujolais is simpler. Here the base of the pyramid is plain Beaujolais; next up is a category called Beaujolais Villages, from a largish group of communes that aren't individually named, and top are the wines of the ten Beaujolais *cru* villages,

St-Amour, Juliénas, Chénas, Chiroubles, Regnié, Fleurie, Morgon, Brouilly, Côte de Brouilly, and Moulin-à-Vent. These rarely if ever carry the name Beaujolais.

Aligoté

This grape variety has been called "Burgundy's Muscadet" – meaning that it's an inexpensive, fresh-tasting wine that's perfect with seafood. It appeals either to those who know a lot about wine, or those who know nothing but appreciate a good drink. If you're looking for oaky, exaggerated aromas you'll be disappointed – Aligoté smells of apples or lemons. Even world-famous growers with great vineyard sites often keep a small patch of old Aligoté vines, even though they could make far more money by replanting with Chardonnay.

Burgundy has one village dedicated to Aligoté: Bouzeron in the Côte Chalonnaise (see p.100), where its great champion is Aubert de Villaine, who elsewhere makes one of the world's most expensive and sought-after red wines at Domaine de la Romanée-Conti (see p.67)

Good examples of Aligoté include Ghislaine et Jean-Hugues Goisot from St-Bris-le-Vineux (see p.50), and Cave de Bailly (see p.52); Rémi Rollin from Pernand-Vergelesses (see p.81); and Domaine A. et P. de Villaine from Bouzeron.

Chardonnay

The name of the world's most famous grape variety is also the name of a village in the Mâconnais in southern Burgundy, where the wine, not surprisingly, is made from... Chardonnay. It's quite common now for people to say "I don't like Chardonnay", and even "I don't like Chardonnay but I do like Chablis" – even though Chablis is made entirely from the Chardonnay grape.

I find the nearest thing in this region to the round-tasting, so-called "fruit-driven" international Chardonnay style actually comes from Beaujolais (see p.121) where most of the wine is red, but where there's also a little white.

As usual in France, it's a question of the soil. In Beaujolais, the soils are largely acidic or neutral. In Chablis, the Côte d'Or, and the Mâconnais, the vines grow on alkaline limestone soils, which gives them a kind of bracing, mineral quality – what the growers call "*mineralité*". It's possible to become almost moralistic about these white wines, and use contemptuous terms like "flabby" about one not grown in the proper soil.

Of course there's a whole spectrum of wines that can come from the Chardonnay/limestone combination, from a crisp Chablis at one extreme, to the sweet wines Jean Thevenet makes in the Mâconnais, using a proportion of a local type of Chardonnay, Chardonnay Musqué, that produces distinctively

exotic aromas. In the middle there are wines made using the techniques exported to the rest of the world, such as lees-stirring and malolactic fermentation (see p.33), that give the familiar toast and butter notes.

ABOVE *Chardonnay grapes in Burgundy can be grown to optimum ripeness without ever losing the necessary balancing acidity.*

Chardonnays to try
Some examples: in Chablis (see p.44), William Fevre makes Chablis that exemplifies "minerality". In Maranges (see p.93), Domaine Chevrot has decided to make big-flavoured modern-type Chardonnay. In Montagny (see p.107), where Stephane Aladame is based, we're more than 160km (99 miles) south of Chablis, but the wines are again buzzing with the liveliness of limestone soils. In Mâcon (see p.108), Hubert Laferrere from Lugny exemplifies the Mâconnais ultraripe school.

LEFT *Nuits-St-Georges' other claim to fame.*

Crémant
Champagne can be disappointing, but perhaps because it's priced as a treat we tend to drink it with care – properly chilled and with a sense of expectation. Crémant de Bourgogne can appear halfway to cider (apologies to good cider-makers) –

underflavoured and unappetizingly orangey rather than straw-yellow, and with big, coarse bubbles. It's cheaper partly because it lacks the magic name, but partly because the costs are lower. Champagne legally has to be aged in the bottle for a minimum of fifteen months, as opposed to nine for *crémant*. Both are grown on alkaline soils – but the most important difference is that in Champagne, sparkling wines are the whole *raison d'être*, whereas in Burgundy, *crémant* is usually a way of using up less ripe grapes from less good sites.

But you can find excellent *crémant* – especially in Rully, down in the Côte Chalonnaise, which is the *crémant* capital. My great *crémant* moment came when tasting at specialist producer Vitteaut-Alberti and finding the ethereal purity that Champagne drinkers look for – the unlikely impression of ascending into a realm of transcendence and spirituality. I sent a text to a friend on the spot and offered to bring back several cases – he replied that it was a kind thought, but that *crémant* wouldn't impress the girls.

Crémants to try

In the Auxerrois, the Crémant specialist is the cooperative at Bailly (*see* p.52), which turns still wine into sparkling for other co-ops throughout Burgundy. Good, but could sometimes be drier for my taste. The Côte d'Or puts most energy into still wine, but try the *crémant* from André and Bernard Labry in Auxey-Duresses (*see* p.88). In the hills above the Côte you can find dedicated specialists such as Denis Fouquerand of La Rochepot. Rully, as mentioned, is where this wine was created – as well as the excellent Vitteaut-Alberti, André Delorme can be very good, especially its pink version. It's also worth trying the small cooperative, a little further south, at Bissey-sous-Cruchaud.

Gamay

Like Chardonnay, this variety shares a name with a Burgundian village – this time a small hamlet in the southern Côte d'Or, next to St-Aubin. But the general view is that Gamay, which is the red Beaujolais grape, has no place further north than Beaujolais, on clay and limestone rather than the largely granite soils where it does so well. In support you could quote the famous edict of Duke Philippe le Hardi of 1395 banning this "fraudulent" ("*déloyault*") variety. The trouble is that Gamay is too tolerant of overcropping. If you make Pinot Noir vines "piss wine", in the vulgar French phrase, the result is pale and unappetizing. Gamay, on the other hand, will make something that looks like wine even when abused by greedy growers.

Patches of old Gamay hang on in the Côte d'Or, but don't command the same affection growers feel for Aligoté. I don't much care for the traditional Gamay-Pinot blend called

WEIRD VARIETIES AND SURVIVALS

West of Chablis, the village of St-Bris makes a well-known **Sauvignon Blanc**, usually a bit more robust than that from the Loire.

Malbec makes dark, rich wine in Cahors, in southwest France, but it was historically grown in Joigny, north of Chablis, and a little has been revived for that town's speciality rosé called *vin gris*.

Pinot Gris is also grown in Joigny, as is the red **Sacy** grape, and both Sacy and **César** can be blended with Pinot in Irancy, the main red wine village of Auxerrois. At Vézélay, between Chablis and Dijon, they have revived **Melon de Bourgogne**, alias the Muscadet of the Loire.

Things are more conventional in the Côte d'Or, but there is a surprising amount of early maturing **Pinot Blanc** grown to help out in years when **Chardonnay** struggles to ripen satisfactorily.

Good examples include the *vin gris* from Alain Vignot, near Joigny, or the Melon de Bourgogne from the Vézélay cooperative.

"Passetoutgrains", but Gamay on its own, sold as Bourgogne Grand Ordinaire can be good, even very good.

Red Beaujolais hardly needs an introduction, but not everyone realizes that the best of these fresh and fruity wines may keep well for some years. The latest trend is to make Beaujolais as if it were burgundy, and to put a particular stress on its seriousness and keeping potential. I'm not 100 per cent convinced that this is the way to go.

Gamay is also the grape of red Mâcon, sold as Mâcon Rouge. It is often coarse, but good ones can be bargains.

Gamays to try

For good, classic-style Beaujolais, try Jean-Marc Monnet in Juliénas. New style "serious" Beaujolais, head to Château des Jacques, owned by the Beaune merchant house Louis Jadot (see p.125). For Côte de Beaune Bourgogne Grande Ordinaire, see Arnaud Ente of Meursault on p.87; vines planted in 1989; for Mâcon Rouge, see Pascal Pauget from Tournus on p.111.

Pinot Noir

If you're more used to drinking red Bordeaux or Australian Shiraz, a lot of red burgundy is going to baffle you. Pinot Noir is one of what are semi-officially classed as "noble" varieties – according to some fans it's the most distinguished of them all – yet at times it struggles to make recognizably red wine. Pinot will rarely give a huge blockbuster red; the secret of understanding it is to concentrate on the way it smells, and on the way it feels in the mouth, which should be rich and silky.

Of all red grape varieties, this must be the one that responds most dramatically to the vineyard site. The villages of the Côte d'Or are often described as making "masculine" red wines – like, for example, Morey-St-Denis – or "feminine" ones, like neighbouring Chambolle-Musigny. Merchants making red burgundy often buy from villages that produce different styles – say chewy, tannic Maranges, and light Hautes-Côtes de Beaune, and blend them. If you're buying from growers you

ABOVE *A sorting table (actually a conveyor belt) in action. Using it to check every bunch coming into the winery is essential these days for ambitious producers.*

won't have this option (unless you have ambitions to create your own special blend) so it's important to ask if the wine needs maturing to be at it's best. I find that even lighter wines can benefit from ageing, and the flavours that result sometimes remind me of some of the tastes and smells of a patisserie shop: cherry, roasted almond, cream, mocha.

Pinots to try

In the Auxerrois (*see* p.50), you can find excellent Pinot Noir as far north as Chablis. In the Tonerrois (*see* p.41), try Céline Coté in the village of Molosme. Some of the best value in the Côte de Nuits is in the appellation Côtes de Nuits-Villages (*see* p.66), try Gachot-Monnot. Santenay and Maranges (*see* p.91) are also good places to look. Joblot in Givry (*see* p.99) is sought-after, and isn't really cheap, but is still a bargain; the same is true of the wines of Juillot in the neighbouring Côte Chalonnaise village of Mercurey.

Rosé

RIGHT *A culture of all-day drinking often necessitates a midday nap.*

BELOW *Vines on the Hautes-Côtes, Burgundy's high-altitude vineyards where Pinot Noir in cooler years struggles to make well-coloured wines.*

Given that Pinot Noir makes such pale wine, you'd think it would be a natural to make rosé; but only one village, Marsannay, just south of Dijon, has really made a name for this style. There is some quite drinkable Gamay rosé in the Mâconnais region.

In Epineuil (*see* p.41), Dominique Gruhie makes a rosé in the same way as they do in the village of Les Riceys, just across the border in the Champagne region, where the rosé is one of France's most celebrated.

Wine culture:
the art of serious drinking

In France, unlike in some other countries, wine is a source of pleasure – not a reason for confusion, embarrassment or one-upmanship. If you don't feel you know much about the subject, it might seem stressful to try to exercise your taste and judgement in front of people who've practically been weaned on the stuff. So bear in mind that French wine culture – in Burgundy at any rate – does not involve preciousness or pretentiousness.

Wine as a way of life

The first thing to understand is that – even after years of anti-alcohol campaigns – the French drink an awful lot. If you go for a morning coffee in one of the cafés on the cathedral square in Chalon-sur-Saône you may well be outnumbered – especially on a market day – by workers starting the day with their traditional *p'tit coup de blanc* (small white wine). White wine is considered to have the same energizing properties we associate with coffee, so later in the day, or at mealtimes, they will switch over to red. French drinkers don't usually get drunk, but they do aim to stop their blood alcohol ever falling below a certain level. Just read any Maigret novel – M. le Commissaire's trail invariably leads him through bars and cafés where he can grab a steady succession of glasses of beer, wine, and calvados.

The way wine is served is also unfussy. Few bother with the goldfish-bowl glasses that have become fashionable in America – most tasting is done with what looks like a small brandy glass. Smoking isn't considered to interfere with wine appreciation; most of Beaune's blenders in the past smoked the local black tobacco cigarettes.

The growth of wine-speak

In both France and the rest of the world, wine-speak is quite a new invention. Much of it actually comes from this region, and was the creation of Jules Chauvet (see p.122), the Beaujolais

FROM THE MEMOIRS OF FAMED BURGUNDIAN-BORN NOVELIST, COLETTE (1873–1954)

"There is something very mysterious about vines, and about wine. In the whole plant kingdom, only the vine interprets the earth and its flavours – and so faithfully, too. The vine seeks out the secrets of the soil, and its grapes gives them expression. Flint, through the medium of the vine, tells us that it is something living, soluble, nourishing. Coarse chalk, as wine, sheds tears of pure gold."

"He knew that when he left
he would not be able to
resist **his longing to go
and drink a glass at the
Caves du Beaujolais.** For
one thing, he really liked
the atmosphere of that sort
of little café, where you
see many people and the
proprietor chats to you
familiarly.

He liked Beaujolais too,
particularly when, as here,
it was served in little
earthenware jugs.... [later]
he went across the bridge
with the pleasant, rather
rough, taste of Beaujolais
in his mouth."

**All this was considered
a bit strong for public
sensibilities back in 1960s
Britain.** When the Maigret
stories were adapted for
BBC television at that time
(according to Simenon's
biographer Patrick
Marnham), a temperance
pressure group recorded
the amount the detective
drank in each episode
and a Church of England
bishop pleaded that it
should be reduced.

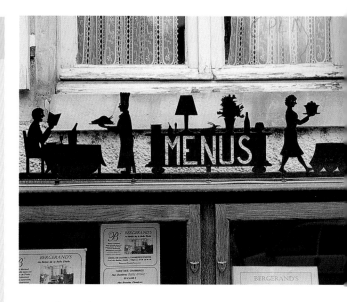

winemaker and wine merchant who helped create the standard
modern tasting glass, and who analysed the aromas of wine
into a series of family groups: floral, fruit-related, animal/meaty,
and so on. But long before Chauvet, people talked about wines
in terms of other scents and flavours: may-blossom, honeysuckle,
hay, morello cherries, and so on.

Some of them develop a personal language – in grower
Dominque Lafon's case, a kind of body language. Lafon does
a sudden karate chop combined with a short whistle to convey
the ideas a British wine merchant would put across with words
like "raciness", "minerality", and "backbone" (it's all the
opposite of "flabby").

How young and how cool?

People often say that the French drink wine without the long
cellaring others go in for. This is true in that ninety per cent of
the wine they buy is everyday stuff. But many do have cellars,
and it is widely appreciated that some wine needs time; in
particular it would be considered wrong to pay more than €10
for a *premier cru* (see p.17) burgundy and then drink it without
the two or three years it will need to show at its best.

Decanting and serving temperatures: the simple rule is that
red burgundy usually needs to be cooler than you might expect,
and white a little less cold. The Beaujolais region is sensibly
using its promotion budgets to tell drinkers to try their red wine
chilled. Most red burgundy doesn't need decanting unless it's a
grand old bottle full of sediment. On the other hand whites –
especially top quality ones – do open up with decanting.

How to get there

F or most Europeans, Burgundy is the most easily accessible French region. Beaune is just two hours by car from Geneva, five hours from Brussels, Frankfurt or Milan, and even from London the journey takes little more than eight hours, including some waiting around to cross the Channel. By rail it can be even faster: with the TGV and Eurostar it's possible to leave Burgundy and be back in London before midday. Dijon airport was briefly opened up for passenger use by the KLM-owned low-cost airline Buzz. This service – understandably popular with the professional wine buyers – was discontinued in 2003 when Ryanair bought up Buzz. It's possible that Ryanair or another carrier might revive it; in the meantime Lyon airport is a poor substitute, and St-Etienne, where Ryanair flies, is even further from Burgundy.

Going by road

Drivers coming from Calais or from Brussels have to decide early whether to take the crowded A1 motorway via Paris, or to follow the A26 on its eastward meander via Reims.

If you want to visit Chablis, Vézélay, and the Auxerrois en route, there's no alternative to Paris. Try to make sure you do this part of the journey outside rush hours, at a time when the capital's inadequate ring road, the N104 La Francilienne (otherwise known as the Périphérique) isn't gridlocked.

Psychologically, the advantage of the Paris route is that the long drive through France is broken into manageable segments. Reims gives the same sense of a staging point on the

LEFT *Restaurants in Burgundy are often husband and wife affairs, as celebrated here in silhouette.*

BELOW *Growers curse the TGV high-speed train when it slices through their vineyards, as here, west of Mâcon.*

FAR RIGHT *The Accor group has become one of the world's top ten hotel chains.*

BELOW *There are campsites all over – lists from Offices de Tourisme plus other local tips.*

DO FRENCH DRIVERS MAKE YOU NERVOUS?

You are right to be afraid. **France had the worst accident rate** in the pre-enlargement EU after Portugal. But although they can be scary, **the autoroutes are much safer than the old Routes Nationales,** where the authorities recently launched a programme to remove roadside trees because so many drivers crashed into them.

Don't waste nervous energy getting angry when you are tailgated at 140km/hr (87 mph). Behind the wheel the French are individualists and the driver flashing his lights at you expects you to be equally pig-headed.

If you can't beat them, adopt some non-lethal French habits, such as keeping your indicator on in the overtaking lane, speeding up, within reason, and relieving your frustrations with an occasional cry of *"putain"* or *"connard".*

A26-A5-A31 route, together with a brief but heart-lifting view of its cathedral, a war-scarred gothic masterpiece. You also have the option of shopping for Champagne, either in the Reims-Epernay heartland or, more enterprisingly, in the lesser known Aube.

Beware the breathalyser

Remember, when driving in France, that the French limit for alcohol in the blood is five milligrammes per millilitre.

The joys of service stations

Although it's tempting to get the journey over as quickly as possible, for safety's sake it's vital to stop every couple of hours. Some people think France's motorway service stations are a disgrace. I wouldn't go quite so far; nor, I think, would anyone who has ever stopped at a British motorway service station. For a long time I used to break the journey at Sommesous, the next *aire de service* after Reims-Champagne, partly because I was fascinated by its automated massage chairs, but the next one south, at Troyes-Fresnoy-le-Château, currently gets my vote. Service stations often sell wine, both in the food section and the gift-shop, but it will be overpriced négociant stuff.

Where to stay

To work through all the itineraries in this book would take more than a normal-length holiday. So some selection is required. It's simple if you're just passing through the region: interesting wine producers can be reached from every part of the A6 Paris-Lyon motorway – usually with a fifteen minute diversion, at most an hour. But how should you plan a visit of a week or a fortnight specifically devoted to Burgundy and its wines?

Early decisons

One easy principle is to break the holiday into two contrasting halves. You could include a wine-free period, visiting fascinating places that fall outside the scope of this book, like Autun (25km/15 miles west of Couches, see p.93), with its Roman gate and amphitheatre and a cathedral with some of the world's greatest Romanesque art.

If you plan to visit growers every day, perhaps settle on two contrasting types of wine you'd like to bring home: inexpensive reds (from Beaujolais) and classic whites (from Chablis). Or you could mix a tour through some very well-known wine villages with some completely unknown ones. I've tried to do this even within individual itineraries – for example in the famous Côte d'Or there are suggested trips to the underrated valley of the Saône and the little-known places at the top of the Hautes Côtes.

Burgundy isn't a place for generalisations, but if you want to come home with your favouirte wines: look for light, fruity, scented wines from Chablis and the other northern vineyards; "proper", well-coloured red wines from the Côte de Nuits and also from Maranges and the southern end of the Côte d'Or; an interesting mixed grab-bag including sparkling wines in the Côte Chalonnaise; and some almost New World-type Chardonnays in the Mâconnais.

A little luxury

Mix and match too when choosing a place to stay. Especially in under-priced regions like Beaujolais and the Auxerrois – growers often double up as gîte-keepers. But think of all the money you're saving by buying direct, and consider allowing yourself a night or two in a château (e.g. see p.82 and 120) and/or a meal in a three star restaurant (see p.42 and 97).

Growers and négociants

F rench wine labels tell you the vintage and the wine's region or village of origin (*see* p.17). But one of the most useful bits of information comes in small letters along the bottom of the label. This begins with the words *"Mis en bouteille par..."* ("bottled by...") and it tells you who made the wine, and, perhaps as importantly, what kind of producer they are. For some years the most prized description has been *"propriétaire-récoltant"* (wine-grower, literally "owner-grower"), or the variants *"vigneron"* and *"viticulteur"*, which mean the same thing. The label will also tell you where the grower is based, with the postcode, and sometimes the telephone number.

ABOVE *A Burgundy village can be home to scores of individual growers.*

RIGHT *This vineyard, with its landmark sign, is owned by Patriarche, the Beaune-based négociant.*

Finishing school

Many bottles will say something like *"Elevé et mis en bouteille par..."* The key word is *"Elevé"*, which can mean "educated", "bred" or "brought-up" – but in wine terms refers to blending and maturing. If the bottler is only taking responsibility for this part of the process, it is almost certainly a merchant house, a "maison", "négociant" or "négoce", one of the old establishments traditionally based in Beaune or Nuits-St-Georges.

Are growers always better?

Is more good wine made by growers who do the bottling themselves, or by the négociants? Whenever I've tasted growers' wines against equivalently priced merchants' wines, the growers have impressed me as making something more individual and memorable. But they will have been the elite picked out as worth importing. It may be that overall the merchants get a more consistent result. However, for around seventy years it's been the best growers that have set wine buffs' pulses racing, from the Marquis d'Angerville in Volnay, Leflaive in Puligny-Montrachet, and Armand Rousseau in Gevrey-

Chambertin in the 1930s, to Henri Jayer of Vosne-Romanée in the 1970s, and more recently names such as Denis Mortet in Gevrey-Chambertin or Vincent Girardin in Santenay.

Wine is an extremely complicated subject, especially in Burgundy, and for a while "growers = good, négociants = boring" offered a rule of thumb, even though it was hugely unjust to the great work that continued to be done at the best négociants, large and small.

When growers become négociants

Now the distinction has started unravelling. The ultimate cause for the blurring of the boundaries is the lack of land for sale in Burgundy, particularly on the Côte d'Or. When growers find they've become cult names, they naturally want to expand, but are frustrated because there's nothing to buy.

The alternative is to buy, not land, but grapes from other growers, and to take out the négociant's licence required by the French state. As well as growers who've expanded, there are also several excellent examples of new, small-scale négociants. Meanwhile the merchant houses have been alarmed both by the numbers of growers who are bottling their wine rather than selling it to them, and by the competition for those that remain. Their solution is to use their corporate resources to turn themselves into vineyard owners – witness, for example, the Beaune merchants Louis Jadot's big purchases of Beaujolais estates (see p.125).

RISING AND RISEN STARS – GROWERS

New star growers emerge amazingly fast. Three who were being fêted at the time of writing were **Vincent Dancer** of **Chassagne-Montrachet** (see p.85), **Jean-Marc Vincent** in **Santenay** (see p.92) and **François Raquillet** of **Mercurey** (see p.103), but they'll probably be a) old hat and b) very expensive indeed by the time you get to read this book.

BELOW *The major co-op in Pouilly-Fuissé.*

RIGHT *Unloading grapes at Louis Jadot, mid-harvest.*

RISING AND RISEN STARS – NEGOCIANTS

. . . .

TRADITIONAL LARGE NEGOCIANTS:
Three of the best are, from north to south, **Faiveley** in Nuits-St-Georges (see p.67); **Bouchard Père et Fils** (not to be confused with the similarly named Bouchard Ainé et Fils) in Beaune (see p.74); and **Rodet** in Mercurey (see p.102). There is also the well-known **Duboeuf** in Beaujolais (see p.125).

GOOD, SMALL NEGOCIANTS:
Beaune is home to two, both run by Americans: the new **Maison Alex Gambal**, and the very old **Camille Giroud**, the latter now managed by Beaune's most influential American expat, Becky Wasserman. (The large and famous **Maison Louis Jadot**, incidentally, is American-owned but French-run.) And, Beaujolais has two outstanding small négociants: **Trenel** at Charney-lès-Mâcon, and **Pierre Ferraud** in Belleville (see p.129).

MINI-NEGOCIANTS:
François d'Allaines in Demigny (see p.91), and **Olivier Merlin** in La Roche Vineuse, near Mâcon (see p.116), are both very good indeed.

The role of the courtier

But the picture is still more complicated. If you visit enough growers you will probably run into a member of another of the wine business' tribes, a "courtier". This is not a flunkey, but a middleman or broker, who finds buyers for the growers and sources of supply for the négoce.

Cooperatives: good, bad or indifferent?

Then there are the *caves cooperatives*, the growers' cooperatives – a movement that, like estate bottling, was a product of the tough years of the 1930s. Expensive wines have scarcity value, and most co-ops make a lot of wine and so lack prestige. They therefore tend to be coy about announcing themselves on the label, almost never stating "cooperative" and preferring terms like "*Cave de...* such and such a village" or "*Les vignerons réunis de...*". One of them has annoyed independent growers by using the phrase "*Mis en bouteille à la propriété*", which sounds misleadingly like a single estate wine.

There are some dedicated people working in cooperatives, but their difficulty lies in persuading growers to take real pride in providing grapes whose individual identity will be submerged in the mass. Most co-ops are in the Mâconnais, and produce inoffensive white burgundy, much of which ultimately appears under négociants' names.

The smallest co-op, in Vézélay (see p.55) is probably also the best in the region.

How Burgundians make wine

Y ou don't have to know much about winemaking techniques to appreciate wine, any more than you need a knowledge of classical sonata form to listen to Beethoven or the Beach Boys. And one refreshing fact is that almost every decent grower in this region believes that the less "winemaking" you do, the better.

Keep it simple

Wine begins as gardening and ends as a sort of cooking. Good cooks take the best possible materials and present them to their best advantage. Similarly the grower aims to produce well-flavoured grapes, harvest them at the point of perfect ripeness, and then to put them into a kind of suspended animation through fermentation.

Of all fruit, grapes offer the perfect starting point. They're juicy, and so are immediately ready (unlike, say, barley) for conversion by the yeasts on their skins and in the air. These micro-organisms can survive in levels of alcohol that poison rival bugs. Grapes also contain tartaric and malic acid, which further discourage spoilage by bacteria, and contain tannins in their skins (red grapes in particular) and stalks: chemicals that are a natural preservative. As the alcohol levels rise the yeasts die off – but their remains continue to guard their legacy, by acting as natural antioxidants, preventing air contact from spoiling the wine while it's in barrel.

White wine: press first

White winemaking starts with pressing the grapes, and it's normal in Burgundy to press whole bunches (in some regions it's common to remove the stems and crush them first), so that the stalks act as a sort of natural filter. To press whole bunches means harvesting by hand – harvesting machines shake the individual grapes off their stems. The juice can be settled to clear it from the gunk the French call the "bourbes", before it is fermented either in large vats or smaller oak barrels.

Red wine: keep the skins

Red grapes produce white juice (much white Champagne is made from red Pinot Noir grapes), so to get red wine you need to extract the colour from the skins. Traditional Burgundian winemaking involves putting the whole bunches of grapes into open vats, then climbing in and treading them to liberate the juice and squeeze colour from the skins. The treading is called "pigeage", and it's a matter of judgement how often to do it,

ABOVE *Heat is needed in barrel-making to bend the staves. It also chars the wood to create the "toasty" character that can make – or mar – modern wines.*

RIGHT *Rotary fermenters are often the sign of industrial winemaking, but not here at Domaine Joblot.*

just as when using a tea bag you judge from the colour of the tea whether and how much to squeeze it with a spoon. *Pigeage* can also be done with poles, or the process can be mechanized, as you can see for example in the huge vats at the cooperative at Buxy in the Côte Chalonnaise (*see* p.106).

Pigeage is quite a violent process. They don't use it in Bordeaux, where the local grape varieties, Cabernet Sauvignon and others, are deeper coloured than Pinot Noir. Instead they pump wine from the bottom of the vat to the top. Another increasingly popular technique, called *délestage*, involves draining the tank, leaving only the *marc*, the pressings debris, and then returning the wine. Yet another possibility is to use mechanical rotary fermenters, which look a little like giant front-loading washing machines. These can make very harsh wines, but at Domaine Joblot in Givry (*see* right) they swear that if the rotations are used sparingly they give excellent results. Red wine, unlike white wine, is pressed after fermentation.

Extracting colour and flavour

Tea gets stronger the longer you leave the teabag in. Similarly, the character of red wine depends on the length of maceration. You can soak the grapes before and after fermentation. Most modern winemakers like to remove the stems (which can take away from the fresh, fruity flavours of the grapes), and chill the lumpy purée of juice and skins for a week or more before allowing the fermentation to start. One of the pioneers of this approach, the consultant Guy Accad, advocated quite high doses of sulphur dioxide (SO$_2$ – the winemaker's all-purpose disinfectant). SO$_2$ is powerfully effective in extracting colour, and making deep-coloured wines. Another influential winemaker, Henri Jayer, used a less extreme "cold soak" without the high SO$_2$. Soaking grapes in juice, as opposed to new wine, doesn't result in a deep colour, but it does extract what they French call "*matière*" – the rich and complex mixture of flavouring elements that is the building material of great wine.

Beaujolais, by the way, has its own distinctive red wine techniques, which are described on p.129.

Winemakers can use all sorts of tricks to make something that's "*flatteur*" – "flattering" or crowd-pleasing. There's the role of oak barrels, for example. When new, these can add notes of toast and vanilla.

Stirring the lees

Then there is *bâtonnage*, which involves poking a stick into a barrel of maturing wine (usually white, but increasingly red as well) and stirring up the dead yeast cells, the "lees". Originally this was a way of kicking off a secondary bacterial fermentation (called the malolactic fermentation) which, as the name implies, softens any malic acid into its less aggressive cousin, lactic acid. But a side effect is to give the wine a richer texture and make it more aromatic.

How can you tell if a winemaker is likely to be conscientious? France's wine critics have codified what they expect: *see box, right*, headed Dogma, in homage to *Dogme 95*, the Copenhagen *cinéastes* who set out a ten-point "vow of chastity" to "rescue" film-making from artifice.

DOGMA – THE TEN RULES OF WINEMAKING

1. Do not use **single-clone vines**, but a selection of naturally diverse plants.

2. Plough to suppress **weeds** rather than use herbicides.

3. **Limit yields** to ensure well-flavoured grapes. Do this by pruning in spring, not by removing excess berries.

4. Harvest **by hand**.

5. **Press white grapes immediately**, and do not attempt to add flavour by allowing contact between the juice and the skins.

6. Allow the juice – the "must" – to **clear naturally**, without using pectolytic enzymes, which give an artificial flavour.

7. Ferment using **natural ambient yeasts**, not with commercial single strains. Do not use these strains to create an artifical flavour.

8. Use barrels because of their physical properties, not to add an **oaky flavour**.

9. **Chaptalize** (add sugar) to a minimal extent and do not add tartaric acid.

10. **Filter** the wine to a minimal extent and do not cold-stabilize it.

Many Burgundians are certified organic, or follow organic principles without declaring it on their labels.

The etiquette of visiting wine-growers

I n France it can be rewarding to stay in a *gîte* or a *chambre d'hôte;* on the other hand, sometimes you feel that a hotel is less hassle. There's a similar trade-off when deciding whether to buy direct from a grower or to go to a shop. I find that dealing directly with growers transforms both the simple transaction of buying wine, and the experience of being on holiday. But to avoid potential embarrassment and misunderstandings, there are points to watch.

Culture clashes

Some French country people, like their equivalents elsewhere, have a parochial view of other cultures. Couples I know with mixed-race children have told me that they've encountered, not racism, but a sort of clumsy gaucheness. Don't be deterred.

However, the easiest mistake for anyone to make is to arrive unannounced during a meal. Do be deterred from this. The hours from midday to 1.30pm are pretty much off-limits. In general it's best to ring first to make an appointment.

"Bonjour, monsieur"

The *vigneron* will probably only speak French, although very frequently there is someone else in the family – often a teenage or grown-up son or daughter – who will be fluent in another language. But it's a simple situation: so long as you know that "*un rendez-vouz*" is "an appointment", "*une dégustation*" is "a tasting", and that "*gouter*" also means "to taste", and that "*j'aime*" means "I like". If you're hesitant in French, my tip would be to concentrate on the formalities that go down so well: shaking hands, smiling, saying "*bonjour*", "*si'il vous plait*", and "*merci*" and – and this is important – endlessly calling people by their titles: "*bonjour*" is good, but "*bonjour, monsieur*" is much better.

Finding the place

Usually the property will be *fleché* (signposted) and there will also be a *panneau*, a signboard. If completely stuck, make for the church or the war memorial (every village has these), ring on your mobile, and say you're lost and beside the *église* or the *monument aux morts*, and ask them to come and get you. Do try to make sure you end up with the grower you intended. Certain surnames re-appear endlessly: Gros, Magnien, Morey, Prunie…. It's easy to end up with the wrong one, though you may stumble on an undiscovered superstar.

Tasting the wines

How many wines can you taste? One grower once complained to me about being on the itinerary of cycle tours, and being asked to open bottle after bottle with only the remotest prospect of a sale. Ideally you won't spend all your time in the tasting area (*le caveau*) but will be taken to see the presses, the fermentation area (*les chais*), and the cellar full of barrels (*les caves de maturation*). A good sign is lots of small fermentation tanks rather than a few big ones: this shows that the grower is concerned to process his different patches of land, his *parcelles*, separately to bring out the individuality of each one.

Growers will usually have at least one or two open bottles for tasting; perhaps stick to these until or unless you become convinced you want to buy in quantity (say at least six bottles). If you hate the wine, indicate that you're doing a complete tour of local producers before returning to purchase and bow out ("*J'ai d'autres producteurs à visiter, mais peut-être que je reviendrai.*" ("I have lots of other growers to see but perhaps I can come back later.")

But, unless you really hit it off with a grower, it's best to taste your way across a big range of wines elsewhere. Other possibilities are the Maisons du Vin run collectively by the region's producers in Chablis, the Côte Chalonnaise, the

BELOW *Bernard Royet and son Jean-Claude in the Côtes du Couchois (see p.95). In Burgundy becoming a regular customer usually means getting to know a family.*

BELOW *This beauty spot is good value, with the producer at La Rochepot (see p.97).*

USEFUL WORDS AND PHRASES

"Bonjour monsieur/ madame."

"Je voudrais déguster quelque chôse, s'il vous plaît." ("I should like to taste something, please.")

"Non, juste ce que vous avez d'ouvert." ("No, whatever you have open.")

"Merçi monsieur/ madame."

After the wine's poured, you may be asked *"Ça vous plaît?"* ("Do you like it?") It's quite enough to nod and smile.

"On pourrait faire un petit tour pour voir vôtre chai?" Growers will want to show you round the winery.

"Qu'est-ce que vous avez içi comme surface en hectares?" ("How big is the estate?") You will then be told what they own and in which appellations.

"Est-ce que vous avez une liste de vos prix?" They will have a price list.

When leaving: *"Au revoir, monsieur, madame."* And you can add *"Bonne journée"* ("Have a good day"), *"Bonne soirée"* (if it's getting late), and if they're about to eat – they often are – *"Bon appetit!"*

Don't worry though, there's often an English-speaker lurking somewhere.

Mâconnais, and Beaujolais. Alternatively the bigger co-ops, like Buxy or La Chablisienne, are more than happy to give tastings to visitors.

Giving an opinion

Now comes the tricky part. You are concentrating on the wine (which you should always spit out, if you can bear to, it looks much more professional). But the grower is concentrating on you. Months, no, years, of labour have gone into what's in your glass. What do you think about it?

With experience you will realize that the best reaction is honesty. Broadly speaking, wine can be more or less *concentré*, *fruité*, *minerale* or *florale*. You can also pick up animal notes (leather or game) in older wine. A very French word is *torrefaction* – the scorched smell of roast coffee – though this is more common in Bordeaux or the south than here. It doesn't matter if you disagree with the grower – "all tasters are right, even when they're wrong", according to one French wine writer. If you're at a total loss, however, two useful gambits are a) to write some kind of note, no matter what. The grower won't be able to read it, and it's a distraction; and b) to ask the grower what he or she thinks, perhaps by saying *"Parlez un peu de ce vin, s'il vous plait"*.

To buy or not to buy?

If you like the wine, what should you buy? The temptation is to stock up on too much top-of-the-range stuff, which will probably need cellaring for a year or more to show at its best, and not to get enough wine to drink immediately. As a rough rule of thumb, try to force yourself to buy seventy-five per cent regional or village appellation wines (like Mâcon Blanc, or Chablis, or Bourgogne Rouge or Aligoté),

which means buying nine basic bottles for three *premiers crus*. Otherwise you'll end up drinking your expensive bottles long before they're ready.

Finally: paying for it. Do not assume that the grower will be equipped for card payments. Even worse, don't present a card that for any reason fails to clear: with France's peculiar financial culture you will be regarded as a would-be fraudster. So make sure you've visited a *distributeur* (a cash machine).

Time out from wine

Even people who make their living from wine get gripped by the urge to drink beer, or to go out dancing. Here are some of my favourite other things to do in Burgundy.

Eat out
Hardly an escape from wine, of course. Many cheap and first-rate restaurants are listed in this book. If you're still obsessed, the wine list will also suggest possibilities for follow-up visits. Two worrying tendencies: the rise of pizza, which in France tends to be too gooey, with unorthodox ingredients such as frogs' legs (I'm not joking), and also the arrival of pretentious *nouvelle cusine* instead of classic stuff such as *oeufs en meurette* (eggs in red-wine sauce) and *boeuf bourguignonne*.

ABOVE *Stop for honey – almost as much fun as wine.*

Go swimming
The French insist on 50m (164-foot) pools and there are fewer reasons for lane rage than in Britain.

BELOW *If a restaurant is busy and the customers are local, you won't be disappointed.*

Buy honey
The countryside here is rich in the wild flowers that have too often been obliterated elsewhere by spraying, and gifted artisans make a wide range of honeys, often showing the same urge to capture the nuances of their particular terroir as their wine-growing neighbours.

Walk and/or cycle
You experience the sights, sounds, and smells of the countryside to the full, and the exercise balances out any over-indulgence. Ask at local tourist offices for bike hire. There's also a trend to view vineyards by hot air balloon, or *montgolfier* (see p.74)

Visit a market
In particular, the teeming market at Louhans in Bresse (every Monday), with the famous (live) *poulets*, of course, but also geese, rabbits, and so on for the thousands of Burgundians

ABOVE *The Sunday market in Châlon-sur-Saône.*

RIGHT *If you're driving, pack wine carefully to avoid breakages, and keep it as cool as possible.*

BELOW *St-Gengoux-le-National is home to one of France's very best chocolatiers.*

for whom they are something between pets and livestock. Louhans is 32km (20 miles) east of Tournus (*see* map p.109) on the D977. Also excellent cheese and charcuterie.

Go backwards

Immerse yourself in the early middle ages, at Vézélay (*see* p.55), or in the Mâconnais (*see* p.112), for example at Cluny. Burgundy boomed from the tenth century, and is a treasure-house of Romanesque architecture.

Silent nights

The downside of this that from around 10pm the place is dead. Teenagers and young adults may well chafe at all this wholesome living – although, unlike in other countries, they can hire small motorcycles from the age of fourteen and risk their necks in the country lanes.

There are some clubs to be found in the larger towns, and, incongruously plonked in the middle of the vineyards, like the casino which is located in the town of Santenay – at the southern end of the Côte d'Or.

How to get your wine home

It's quite feasible to visit growers on foot, by bicycle, by hired car or even by boat, and to ask them to deliver to a local address. But there is no substitute for your own car for the convenience of being able to load up the boot and not worry about it until you get home. But, when it comes to going through customs, remember that the amount of wine you can carry with you is limited.

The occasional importer

The baggage allowance of the cross-Channel train service Eurostar (tel: [0]8705 186186) is two large items and one small item per person, so you could just about bring home two cases of wine. Eurostar's freight service isn't at present a cost-effective way to transport wine. The lamented airline Buzz was about to launch a ship-your-wine service just before it was bought up. Ryanair has no plans to copy this, but customer pressure might perhaps sway it. If you develop a taste for the wine of a particular grower, you might consider importing their wine directly, and opening an account with a carrier such as Interlink (tel: [0]500 005 005; www.interlinkexpress.com). The carrier will make arrangements to pay the duty (which in the UK is £14.67 per case at the time of writing). You will be what is classed as an Occasional Importer. (For more information call the national advice line on [0]845 010 9000, or consult the website www.hmce.gov.uk/ forms/notices/204.htm.)

Discovering Vineyards in Burgundy

Joigny, Côte St-Jacques, Epineuil, and Tonnerrois

These towns are 64km (40 miles) apart, but for the last 200 years have been joined by the Canal de Bourgogne, which brought their wines to Paris. Their vineyards also share a history of neglect followed recently by a well-deserved revival. We're pretty far north here and late spring frosts can destroy the crop: the solution, as at Chablis, is portable heaters in the vineyards.

Wines and water

Until railways made the south of France accessible, these towns of the Yonne *département* supplied much of the wine for the Parisian market; today as pioneers replant vineyards abandoned since the phylloxera epidemic a century ago, many modern Parisians again come wine-shopping here.

You could combine a visit to both vineyards with a lazy week on a pleasure boat, hired from Locaboat Plaisance in Joigny (*B2*, tel: 03 86 91 72 72; www.locaboat.com). Tie up in Tonnerre and visit the vineyards here and in neighbouring Epineuil by bicycle hired at the Tonnerre campsite in Avenue Aristide Briant (tel: 03 86 55 15 44). Growers will happily motor any purchases to the quayside. A further 9km (5.6 miles) on the canal brings you to the fabulous seventeenth-century château at Tanlay, and Tanlay's equally unmissable restaurant Le Bonheur Gourmand.

What the wines are like

Bargains, in a word: most are little more than €5. And they're not just cheap imitations of more famous burgundies. In Tonnerre the surprise, for wines from vineyards so far north, is that the reds are sometimes so intense. Try the versions from Céline Coté in Vaulichères (*B2*, tel: 03 86 55 47 99), or the admittedly somewhat more expensive, and Biodynamically grown, Cuvée Juliette from Dominique Gruhier in Epineuil (*B1*, tel: 03 86 55 32 51).

LOCAL INFORMATION

Office de Tourisme
4, Quai Henri Ragobert
BP 52
89302 Joigny
Tel: 03 86 62 11 05
www.ville-joigny.fr
ot.joigny@libertysurf.fr

Office de Tourisme
Cellier Place Marguerite
de Bourgogne
89700 Tonnerre
Tel: 03 86 55 14 48
www.tonnerre.fr
ot.tonnerre@wanadoo.fr

BELOW *The Yonne at Joigny, near where it joins the Canal de Bourgogne.*

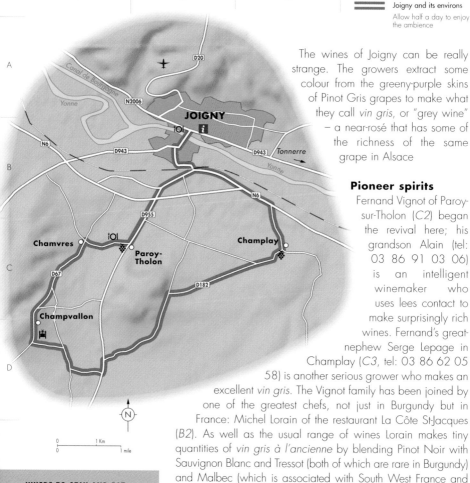

Joigny and its environs
Allow half a day to enjoy
the ambience

The wines of Joigny can be really strange. The growers extract some colour from the greeny-purple skins of Pinot Gris grapes to make what they call *vin gris*, or "grey wine" – a near-rosé that has some of the richness of the same grape in Alsace

Pioneer spirits

Fernand Vignot of Paroy-sur-Tholon (*C2*) began the revival here; his grandson Alain (tel: 03 86 91 03 06) is an intelligent winemaker who uses lees contact to make surprisingly rich wines. Fernand's great-nephew Serge Lepage in Champlay (*C3*, tel: 03 86 62 05 58) is another serious grower who makes an excellent *vin gris*. The Vignot family has been joined by one of the greatest chefs, not just in Burgundy but in France: Michel Lorain of the restaurant La Côte St-Jacques (*B2*). As well as the usual range of wines Lorain makes tiny quantities of *vin gris à l'ancienne* by blending Pinot Noir with Sauvignon Blanc and Tressot (both of which are rare in Burgundy) and Malbec (which is associated with South West France and Argentina, and is even rarer here in Burgundy). Odd.

Survivals

A medieval press in the village of Champvallon, 3km (1.9 miles) south of Joigny (*D1*), has an unbroken record of service. And near Tonnerre, a vineyard planted in 1763 at Bernouil (right, *C4*) is unscathed by phylloxera and still in production.

The Champvallon press is the centrepiece of the village's harvest festivities; it's used by local growers Anne and Rémi Proffit (tel: 03 86 63 50 47), who will know from August 15 onwards the precise day of the party. Otherwise contact the local museum to visit the press (tel: 03 86 91 07 69).

Almost all French vineyards have for many years now been grafted onto phylloxera-resistant American rootstock. But, for some reason, not at La Vigne de l'Empereur, at Bernouil. This vineyard is owned by the Domaine Fournillon-Champeix (34 Grande rue, tel: 03 86 55 50 96). The white wine it produces is rather on the sharp side.

WHERE TO STAY AND EAT

La Rive Gauche
rue Port au Bois
89306 Joigny
Tel: 03 86 91 46 66

Le Moulin
89300 Paroy-sur-Tholon
Tel: 03 86 91 00 63

Château de Vaulichères
89700 Tonnerre
Tel: 03 86 55 02 74

Le Bonheur Gourmand
89430 Tanlay
tel: 03 86 75 82 18

La Côte St-Jacques
89300 Poroy-sur-Tholon
Tel: 03 86 62 06 70

Visiting Joigny

If you're not basing yourself in either town, both are easily reached from Chablis (see the next chapter for suggestions where to stay there). Joigny is more impressive as a whole, with its houses clustered above the Yonne, than for individual buildings – after surviving the Hundred Years' War much was lost in a fire in 1530. But try to see the wood carvings on the half-timbered houses on the street leading between the churches of St Jean and St Thibault, and, near the church of St Jean, the renaissance château of the Italian Gondi family. For good food in Joigny, visit La Rive Gauche – it's more affordable than the Côte St-Jacques.

Tonnerre's underworld

Tonnerre, a much bigger place with eight times Joigny's population, was also the victim of a devastating fire in the sixteenth century. Here don't miss the Fosse Dionne, a basin filled by an underground spring, regarded from Roman times as linked directly to the underworld. More recently it was the town's wash-place or *lavoir*.

You should also visit the nearby Hôtel-Dieu Notre-Dame des Fontenilles, a medieval hospital built in 1293, a century and a half before the more famous example in Beaune (see p.74). The founder was Margaret of Burgundy, the countess of Tonnerre and sister-in-law of the canonised king Louis IX.

For accommodation options, Château de Vaulichères has five *chambres d'hôte*.

GROWERS TO VISIT

Céline Coté at Domaine des Noirots
Vaulichères, 89700 Tonnerre
See main text. (below, B2)

Hervé Dampt
1 rue de Fleys
89700 Comman
Tel: 03 86 55 29 55
(below, B4)

Dominique Gruhier at Domaine de l'Abbaye du Petit Quincy
89700 Epineuil
See main text. (below, B2)

Serge Lepage
9 rue Principale Grand Longueron
89300 Champlay
Tel: 03 86 62 05 58
See main text. (left, C3)

Alain Vignot
16 rue des Prés
89300 Paroy-sur-Tholon
Tel: 03 86 91 03 06
See main text. (left, C2)

PRICES: inexpensive

Tonnere and the Tonnerois
Allow a day to do this at a leisurely pace

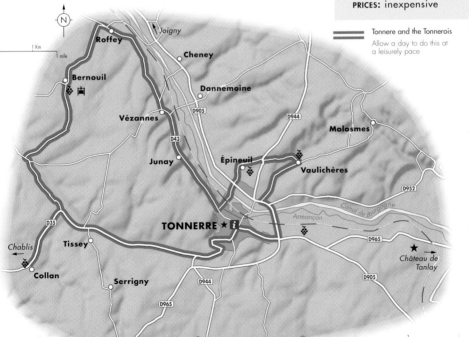

Chablis

C hablis growers are well accustomed to selling wine to returning holidaymakers; their region is only a few minutes' drive from the main autoroute south from Paris. Chablis is rarely as expensive as its equivalent from the Côte d'Or, and should be recognizable for its "mineral" quality, even if the grapes have been overcropped to some degree – and in Chablis over-production is a constant temptation.

Where do you draw the line?

"Burgundy wine" in the early middle ages meant the wine of northern Burgundy: the wines of Chablis and neighbouring Auxerre. Until the fifteenth century Côte d'Or wines were just called "Vin de Beaune". And, Chablis' links with Beaune have been shaky at times: during most of the fifteenth century, the period of Agincourt and Joan of Arc, it was allied to the French king, not to the Burgundian dukes and their English allies.

Five hundred years is of course quite long enough for the place to have sorted out its identity. But, Chablis is only just over the border from the Champagne region. The look of the countryside, with its treeless arable fields, is more like Champagne than Burgundy's heartland.

BELOW Chauferettes *in a Chablis vineyard. These small oil heaters protect against frost.*

Indeed, if you discount the bubbles Chablis has quite a bit in common with Champagne. A lot of Champagne, like all Chablis, is white wine made from Chardonnay grapes, grown on a similarly white soil (in Champagne, chalk; here Kimmeridgian limestone, the stone used to build St Paul's Cathedral in London). Both wines have an exhilarating quality, and both have strong natural personalities.

The landholdings here tend to be far bigger than in other Burgundy regions. Growers are much more likely to use harvesting machines than to pick by hand (*see* box p.49) and few are organic – in contrast, say, to some villages in the Côte d'Or where almost everyone seems to be telling you how (*"on respecte la nature"*).

Like the Mâconnais (*see* p.108) in southern Burgundy, the Chablis trade was, for most of the last 300 years, in the hands of the Beaune merchant houses or négociants. Its position in the region's pecking order remains more or less constant: cheaper than Côte de

Beaune names like Meursault, but with a premium over basic white burgundy from further south. But there is more Chablis available. As wine-drinkers have traded up from generic plonk there's been a boom in demand, and the area under cultivation has grown ten-fold since World War II. Chablis' dilemma has been how to meet the demand without compromising quality and so killing the golden goose. The issue has been putting the region's growers at odds with each other for decades.

A special soil

Chablis' distinct soil type is Kimmeridgian limestone, created from defunct sea creatures some 154–148 million years ago, and named after a bay in Dorset by an eighteenth-century French geologist. The other soil type is Portlandian, named after the peninsula that juts out from the Dorset coast, formed, like Kimmeridgian, in the Upper Jurassic period but two million years later. The difference, very simply put, is that Kimmeridgian contains more clay than Portlandian, which has historically been reserved for the less-valued Petit Chablis appellation.

Over a barrel

Winemakers in Chablis want the taste of their wines to reflect these distinct soil types and the land where their vines are planted. But there is a distinct difference of opinion about how to do this. Bernard Raveneau runs what many think is the greatest estate in Chablis with his brother Jean-Marie. He thinks the wine benefits from ageing in oak barrels – in particular the local 132-litre *feuillette*, a barrel a little over half the size of the usual Burgundian barrel, the 228-litre *pièce*. "We certainly don't want our wines to taste of oak. The point about barrel ageing is to get greater purity of flavours – specifically by exposing the wines to a little oxygen. This makes for wines that age better, and more naturally," he explains.

Domaine Louis Michel's reputation rivals that of Raveneau's, and Jean-Loup Michel is equally convinced that his domaine's wines are all the better from being made and matured entirely in stainless steel containers, with no wood contact whatsoever. He says: "It's very simple: we work without oak in order to preserve the concept of terroir, so that Chardonnay on Kimmeridgian soil can express itself without anything other flavours getting in the way."

Mechanical monsters?

The other issue that divides wine-growers in this region is how to pick the grapes: by hand or using mechanical harvesters? Didier Séguier of Domaine William Fèvre doesn't harvest by machine, even when making simple village Chablis. "Hand harvesting costs twice as much as using harvesting machines,"

THE RISE AND SPRAWL OF THE CHABLIS APPELLATION

1830 870ha of vines around the town of Chablis.

1919 First legal definition of the Chablis vineyard area.

1923 Two legal judgements restrict the Chablis appellation to Chardonnay wines (locally called "Beaunois") grown on Kimmeridgian soil (*see left*).

1938 First decree on Chablis from the Institut National d'Appellations d'Origine (set up in 1935), extending the appellation to all local Kimmeridgian soils.

1976 Two new decrees define Chablis and (generally non-Kimmeridgian) Petit Chablis, and allow virgin areas of woodland to be planted, and even classed as *premier cru* vineyard. Chablis growers split into two associations, one backing and one opposing the vineyard expansions.

1976 1,333ha planted around the town of Chablis.

1997 4,033ha planted around the town of Chablis.

(SOURCE: *paper published in 2000 by Guy Dumas, ENSEAD.*)

Chablis
A day for Chablis and a half
to full day for outlying villages

Chablis Grand Cru

Chablis Premier Cru

Woods

0   1 Km
0   1 mile

he says. "The point of it is to get juice in the best possible condition: machine harvesting means that the juice comes into contact with the grape skins, which is something we'd rather avoid. You can make good wine with harvesting machines, and it makes economic sense, particularly at the level of Petit Chablis. But we're especially interested in exploring the nuances of each individual micro-site in the vineyard; with machine harvesting these tend to be somewhat homogenised."

Meanwhile Benoît Droin, of Domaine Jean-Paul Droin, does a mixture of mechanical and hand harvesting, even at the level of *grands crus*. "With machines we can work all hours, and in particular harvest at night when it's very hot," he explains. "The trucks fill up much more quickly and this means we can get the grapes to the press sooner; to work at this speed with hand harvesters would be much more expensive. When it rains it's difficult to tell harvesters to stop and start, whereas a machine operator can stop at any time. On the other hand you can select more rigorously by hand, and there are sites that aren't suitable for machine harvesting – the steep slopes of some of the *grands crus*, for example."

Tasting wine in town

But regardless of how the wine is made, in Chablis you hardly need to go to the growers: with shops in the centre of town they come to you. La Chablisienne, perhaps Burgundy's best big co-op, has a big new tasting room (8 boulevard Pasteur, tel: 03 86 42 89 89, www.chablisienne.com). The small *grand cru* vineyard of La Moutonne is wholly owned (a so-called *monopole*) by Domaine Long-Depaquit, owned by the négociant Albert Bichot. Long-Depaquit is in a château in the centre of town, (45rue Auxerroise, tel: 03 86 42 11 13).

Domaine Michel Laroche has expanded beyond Chablis to the south of

D124
D
D35   Villy
Lignorelles
D131
la Chapelle-
Vaupelteigne   D131a
C
D91
D131   BORGROS   D216   LES
PREUSES   D150
VAUDÉSIR
GRENOUILLES   Fyé
D965   VALMUR   D35
Poinchy   LES
CLOS
Milly   MONTÉE DE   MONT DE
CHABLIS   TONNERRE   MILIEU   D963
B
D345
VAILLONS
D45
VOSGROS
MONTMAINS   D2
D91   Chichée
D62
A
CHAUME
DE
TALVAT
Courgis

Abbay de
Pontigny
Maligny   D35

LA FOURCHAUME

Fontenay-
près-Chablis

BEAUROY

VAU DE VEY   COTE DE LÉCHET

BLANCHOT

LES FOURNEAUX

Fleys

VAUCOUPIN

N

1   2   3   4

France and Chile. Its shop is just a few streets away, (22 rue Louis Bro, tel: 03 86 42 89 99, www.michellaroche.com). Domaine Jean-Marc Brocard, one of the success stories of the last two decades, is based in the village of Préhy but has a shop (3 place Général du Gaulle, tel: 03 86 42 45 76, www.brocard.fr).

No one has anything but praise for Domaine William Fèvre, especially since its takeover in 1998 by the owners of the Beaune négociants Bouchard Père et Fils. Visit its shop and restaurant (10 rue Jules Rathier, tel: 03 86 42 19 41).

These growers, all in the super-league, will sell direct, though may not be geared up for wine tourism: Domaine Jean-Paul Droin (boulevard de Ferrières, tel: 03 86 42 16 78); Domaine Gérard Duplessis (5 quai de Reugny, tel: 03 86 42 10 35). Domaine Louis Michel et Fils (9–11 boulevard de Ferrières, tel: 03 86 42 88 55) and Domaine Louis Pinson (5 quai Voltaire, tel: 03 86 42 10 26) has very good wines, which are hand-harvested and oak matured. Generally expect to pay €7+ for village Chablis, €10+ for *premiers crus* and €20+ for *grands crus*.

ABOVE *Chablis' inimitable vineyard soil, full of tiny fossils.*

What else to buy in Chablis

Andouillette is Chablis' main food speciality. It sounds nasty: a coarse sausage made with pigs' intestine. Many people regard it as a specialised taste. Buy with confidence from Marc Colin, or his neighbour, the Maison de L'Andouillette, in the town centre, at 3 place Général de Gaulle, and grab one of their leaflets with recipe ideas.

Where to stay

In Chablis itself: the well-known, Michelin-starred restaurant and hotel is l'Hostellerie des Clos. At the other extreme is a former Ibis, now the Hotel aux Lys de Chablis. Between the two is the Au Relais de la Belle Etoile, 4 rue des Moulins (tel: 03 86 18 96 08), in the centre of town near the riverside.

But assuming you have a car, there's no reason not to base yourself in L'Isle-Sur-Serein, forty minutes away to the south, and nearer Avallon and Vézelay.

Le Pot d'Etain deserves its excellent reputation for its food and wine list, and its nine rooms aren't overpriced at around €70. You can also visit Domaine de Mauperthuis, 2km (1.2 miles) to the north in the village of Civry-sur-Serein. For the same kind of price, there's the most superior kind of *gîte*, the Domaine de Ste Anne, really an eighteenth century country estate handy for the northerly motorway exit for Chablis (exit 20).

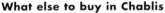

WHERE TO STAY AND EAT

l'Hostellerie des Clos
rue Jules Rathier, 89800 Chablis, Tel: 03 86 42 10 63, www.hostellerie-des-clos

Hotel aux Lys de Chablis,
38 rue Auxerre
89800 Chablis
Tel: 03 86 42 49 20

Le Pot d'Etain
89440 L'Isle-sur-Serein
Tel: 03 86 33 88 10
www.potdetain.com

Domaine de Ste Anne
Soleines le Haut, 89200 Venoy, Tel: 03 86 94 10 16
www.domainesainteanne.com

Charming Hotel Auberge de la Beursaudière
9 chemin de Ronde, 89310 Nitry, Tel: 03 86 33 69 69, www.beursaudiere.com

La Feuillette
rue des Moulins, 89800 Chablis, Tel: 03 86 18 91 67

Le St-Bris
13 rue de l'Eglise
89530 St-Bris-le-Vineux
Tel: 03 86 53 84 56

1   2   3

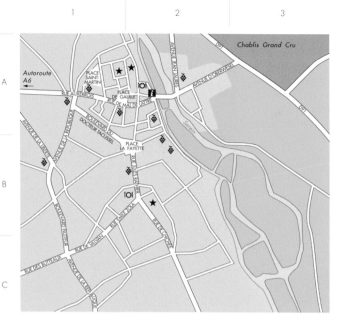

The village of Chablis
Historically, trade here has
been in the hands of the
Beaune merchants or
negociants

BELOW *Riverside Chablis. Some*
excellent producers are based
along these quais.

Near the next exit south, 21, is the quaintly named Charming Hotel Auberge de la Beursaudière.

More affordably, consider looking for a *gîte* or a room in a *chambres d'hôte* (guest house) outside Chablis. There are lists on the Chablis visitors' web page, www.chablis.net.

Destinations for dining include La Feuillette, run by a former member of the staff at l'Hostellerie des Clos. It is good, not pretentious, and not overpriced. Or why not try Le St-Bris, a good, newish, and inexpensive restaurant located in the wine village of St-Bris, 17km (10.5 miles) west of Chablis.

Walking in Chablis

The *grands crus* Bougros, Preuses, Vaudésir, Grenouilles, Valmur, Les Clos, and Blanchot – the seven named vineyards that made Chablis' reputation – all overlook the town from just across the river Serein. It takes barely an hour to leave the town and reach the vantage point of the wood.

A little more ambitiously, you can follow the marked Sentier ("footpath") des Grands Crus for 8km (5 miles) or one of the other nine rather longer routes that have been mapped out by the admirable local walkers' group Les Sentiers Chablisiens (www.sentiers chablisiens.org).

I'm still standing

Chablis has a rather spare, uncluttered feel. This results partly from repeated military devastation by besieging Protestant forces, who burnt Chablis to the ground in February 1568, and by the invading Germans, nearly 400 years later. In June 1940, the Luftwaffe destroyed 100 homes, including medieval buildings that had survived the Huguenots, and bombed and machine-gunned ninety civilians and soldiers.

Surviving monuments include St Martin, the town's parish church. It was one of the first in France in the gothic style, and was begun in 1160 by monks from the Abbey of Tours. Like Canterbury Cathedral it is modelled, albeit on a much smaller scale, on the cathedral at Sens, 80km (50 miles) to the northwest. St Martin is the patron saint of travellers; Joan of Arc is supposed to be one of the many who have sought his protection by nailing a horseshoe to the south door, when she was here in 1429.

Pontigny: where it all began

The twelfth-century cellar of Le Petit Pontigny is the spiritual home of winemaking in Chablis. Viticulture was pioneered, as so often in Burgundy, by Cistercian monks, based in this case at the stupendous abbey of Pontigny, which is 15km (9 miles) away, just past Ligny-le-Chatel in the direction of Joigny. It's France's largest surviving Cistercian abbey church and it dates from the mid-twelfth century – around fifty years after the new order's first monastery was founded at Cîteaux, 12km (7.5 miles) east of Nuits-St-Georges. The early gothic church reflects the austerity of the Cistercians – at odds with the role they played in developing winemaking in Burgundy.

Le Petit Pontigny is now the local headquarters of the Bureau Interprofessionel du Vin de Bourgogne (tel: 03 86 42 42 22), and is the setting for such events as the annual Fête des Vins, on the fourth Sunday in November.

Still with monks and wine, adjoining St Martin is the Obediencerie – monastic buildings, largely dating from the fifteenth and sixteenth centuries, which are currently the headquarters of Domaine Michel Laroche. *See* above, however, for the address of the domaine's shop; this is the place to go for wine sales.

GROWERS IN CHABLIS' OUTLYING VILLAGES

A selection of growers biased in favour of hand-harvesting and organics.

COURGIS:
Domaine J-C. Martin
5 rue de Chante Merle
Tel: 03 86 41 40 33 *(A1)*

Domaine A. et O. de Moor
4 rue Jacques Ferrand
Tel: 03 86 41 47 94 *(A1)*

MILLY:
Domaine Daniel Dampt
17 rue de Champlan
Tel: 03 86 42 47 23 *(B2)*

Domaine D-E. Defaix
23 rue de Champlain
Tel: 03 86 42 42 05 *(B2)*

POINCHY:
Domaine Denis Pommier
31 rue Poinchy
Tel: 03 86 42 83 04 *(B2)*

Domaine Laurent Tribut
15 rue de Poinchy
Tel: 03 86 42 46 22 *(B2)*

LA CHAPELLE-VAUPELTEIGNE:
Domaine de Chantemerle
27 rue du Serein *(C2)*
Tel: 03 86 42 18 95

MALIGNY:
Domaine Olivier Savary
4 chemin des Mates
Tel: 03 86 47 42 09 *(D2)*

FLEYS:
Domaine C. et J-P. Grossot
4 route de Mont-de-Milieu
Tel: 03 86 42 44 64 *(B4)*

Domaine de la Meulière
18 route de Mont-de-Milieu
Tel: 03 86 42 13 56 *(B4)*

PRICES: moderate

Auxerrois

Before phylloxera this was France's single most important wine region; its fortified villages supplied Paris from the provincial capital Auxerre (pronounced "Ausserre") via the river Yonne. Now its fortunes remain mixed, although Irancy and St-Bris have recently been granted their own appellations. The growers of St-Bris have developed a major-league *crémant* business, there are some exceptional growers, and all agree that the vineyards have great potential. Expect some Irancy single vineyards to be granted their own *premier cru* appellations in the future.

Burgundian grapes plus

The usual Burgundian grapes don't have the field quite to themselves here: St-Bris, for example, is made only from Sauvignon Blanc. Some growers aim for an inexpensive version of Loire Sauvignons like Sancerre or Pouilly-Fumé, while others believe that the Kimmeridgean soils they share with Chablis (see p.45) enable them to make something unique: less flinty than Chablis but with more richness and a distinct citrus character reminiscent of lemon mousse. Irancy is the appellation for red wines; here growers have the option of blending the usual Pinot Noir with up to ten per cent of the local César grape, supposedly introduced by the Roman legions. César adds colour at the expense of a certain coarseness. There is Chardonnay, which can be close to Chablis, and a lot of Aligoté, which here can be particularly fruity and aromatic.

BELOW *At least half the buildings in Auxerre's centre seem to be half-timbered.*

A local superstar

The outstanding local producers are the husband-and-wife team of Ghislaine and Jean-Hugues Goisot of St-Bris-le-Vineux. Like the best growers anywhere they make wine that is straightforwardly delicious but which also has great complexity. It's perhaps not a coincidence that they're the first to have brought organic methods to Auxerrois.

"We took over the estate in 1979," says Ghislaine, "and over the years we became concerned about the toxic effects of herbicides and insecticides. Since 1996 we've gone back to ploughing and we've been fully organic since 2001. What we want is something that's concentrated and that has a long future ahead of it. It's difficult to make this approach profitable in appellations that don't sell for a lot of money. Perhaps the more concentrated wines we make can be a little hard to appreciate, but we have a very loyal following."

A curiosity

France's oldest vineyard, and possibly its oddest, takes up 4ha in the middle of a hospital complex in Auxerre. The Clos de la Chainette has an unbroken record of cultivation going back to the seventh century; until the Revolution it was tended by the monks of the neighbouring Abbey of St-Germain. Now it's owned and run by the regional psychiatric hospital; the red and

WHERE TO STAY AND EAT

Office de Tourisme
1–2 quai de la République
89000 Auxerre
Tel: 03 86 52 06 19
www.ot-auxerre.fr
This has a list of *gîtes* and hotels as well as other local information.

Barnabet
14 quai République,
Tel: 03 86 51 68 88
www.jlbarnabet.com

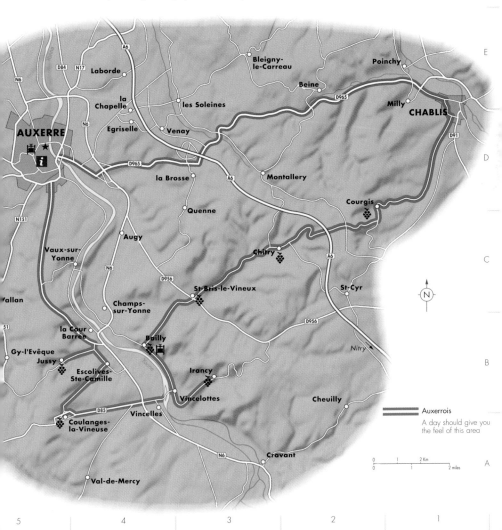

GROWERS IN CHITRY AND ST-BRIS

Bersan et Fils
20 rue du D-Tardieux
89530 St-Bris-le-Vineux
Tel: 03 86 53 33 73 *(C3)*
Try Cuvée Louis Bersan.

Patrick et Christine Chalmeau
76 rue du Ruisseau
89530 Chitry-le-Fort
Tel: 03 86 41 43 71 *(C3)*
Good red Côtes d'Auxerre.

Jocelyne et Philippe Defrance
5 rue du Four
89530 St-Bris-le-Vineux
Tel: 03 86 53 39 04 *(C3)*
Now going organic.

Domaine Ghislaine et Jean-Hugues Goisot
30 rue Bienvenu-Martin
89530 St-Bris-le-Vineux
Tel: 03 86 53 35 15 *(C3)*
See main text.

Olivier Morin
28 rue du Ruisseau
89530 Chitry-le-Fort
Tel: 03 86 41 47 20 *(C3)*
Wines with lively acidity.

Domaine Verret
7 route des Champs
89530 St-Bris-le-Vineux
Tel: 03 86 53 31 81 *(C3)*
The first locally to bottle
their own wine.

PRICES: inexpensive

RIGHT *A vine leaf changing
colour in autumn.*

white wines, which sell for €7 a bottle, are only available by subscription. Apply in writing to M. le Directeur de l'Hôpital Psychiatrique de l'Yonne (4 avenue Pierre Scherer, 89000 Auxerre). For a group visit, contact M. Millière (tel: 03 86 94 39 06). Alternatively try the local restaurants for a taste: La Beursaudière at Nitry (*see* p.48) or Auxerre's own Michelin-starred restaurant, Barnabet.

Visiting the Auxerrois

An itinerary, starting from Chablis, could take in Courgis, then visits to the villages of Chitry-le-Fort, St-Bris-le-Vineux, Bailly, Irancy, Coulanges-la-Vineuse, with the hamlets of Jussy and Migé, and finally Auxerre itself.

Chitry-le-Fort

This village, dominated by the curious church of St Valérien with its fifteenth-century fortifications (four towers and a defensive ditch) lies between the vineyards of Chablis and the Auxerrois. The soils here are dazzling white limestone.

St-Bris-le-Vineux

St-Bris is honeycombed with cellars and underground passages dating from the Hundred Years' War, when Auxerre was held by the English under the Black Prince (1330–76). The description "*le vineux*", announcing its wine-producing status, dates from the Revolution. Surprisingly Sauvignon Blanc, the grape variety that has made the village famous, arrived from the Loire as recently as the 1950s. Make sure you see the church of St-Bris (the name is a corruption of St Priscus, martyred in Rome in AD362, part of whose remains are buried here). Its main treasure is the painting (c.1500) of the tree of Jesse – a visual representation of Christ's genealogy. Across the road, the warren-like cellars of Bersan et Fils give a good flavour of subterranean St-Bris. All the cellars are open on the first Sunday after Bastille Day (July 14) for St-Bris' annual painters' festival.

Taste wine, from St-Bris, and the other Auxerrois and Tonnerois villages, in the Maison du Vignoble Auxerrois (14 route des Champs, tel: 03 86 53 66 76, closed Wednesdays and Sunday mornings).

Bailly

About a kilometre and a half (just under a mile) from St-Bris on the river Yonne is Bailly, where stone was quarried to build Paris from the twelfth century onwards. After the war the St-Bris growers supplied German merchants with still Chardonnay as the base for their sparkling wine. When they lost the contract, they decided to go into business in their own right, using the 5ha of unused underground workings. Various artists have been invited to sculpt their creations into the limestone, and the place is well worth a visit. They also make still wine into sparkling (a process called *élaboration*) for a number of other Burgundy cooperatives, and some of the still white wines are also good.

Irancy
This small pretty village built from Bailly limestone sits in a natural amphitheatre surrounded on all sides by vineyards. There's a specialist wine shop: Chais et Crus (56 rue Soufflot, 89290 Irancy, tel: 03 86 42 33 33).

Coulanges-la-Vineuse
Coulanges has the opposite geography to Irancy: it's on a hill instead of in a sun trap. Perhaps for this reason the wines are pale, but, at best, pleasantly floral. No one here hand-harvests, except for *crémant* (it would be hard to at these prices); what you can hope is that the wine isn't so over-cropped as to be unnecessarily thin. There's a Musée de la Vigne, open most afternoons. Ring the town hall on 03 86 42 20 59.

Don't miss seeing these in Auxerre
Visit the former home of the monks who tended the Clos, at the Abbaye St-Germain (2 place St-Germain, tel: 03 86 18 05 50) in particular to see the extraordinary ninth-century frescoes in the crypt; some of the oldest in France. Also the high gothic Cathedral of St-Etienne with its thirteenth-century stained glass windows, and its eleventh-century murals in the crypt. Make sure you see the view from the tower.

GROWERS IN IRANCY AND COULANGES-LA-VINEUSE

Domaine du Clos du Roi Michel et Denise Bernard
17 rue André Vildieu
89580 Coulanges-la-Vineuse
Tel: 03 86 42 25 72 *(A/B5)*
Reliable.

René Charriat
69 rue Soufflot
89290 Irancy
Tel: 03 86 42 22 21 *(B3)*
Good, old-fashioned wines. The Charriats believe in including some César in their best wine.

Jean-Pierre Maltoff
20 rue d'Aguessea
89580 Coulanges-la-Vineuse
Tel: 03 86 42 32 48 *(A/B5)*
Another good bet.

Michel Martin
61 rue André Vildieu
889580 Coulanges
Tel: 03 86 42 33 06 *(A/B5)*
My favourite grower in Coulanges.

Thierry Richoux
73 rue Soufflot
89290 Irancy
Tel: 03 86 42 21 60 *(B3)*
Richoux hand-harvests, and releases his deep-coloured, long-lived wines at least a year after most of his neighbours.

Pascale et Alain Rigoutat
2 rue du Midi
89290 Jussy
Tel: 03 86 53 33 79 *(B5)*
The village of Jussy is just north of Coulanges on the D463.

PRICES: inexpensive

Vézelay

The twelfth-century abbey church of St Mary Magdalene that dominates the hill village of Vézelay is one of two World Heritage Sites recognized by UNESCO in Burgundy, the other being the Cistercian abbey of Fontenay. Benedictine monks tended and enlarged the existing vineyards at Vézelay, and so created the basis for a wine trade with Paris, via the river Cure. In these vineyards, however, the destruction brought by phylloxera was total – but a revival in the last twenty-five years has created some fine and unusual wines.

LOCAL INFORMATION

Office de Tourisme
12 rue St-Etienne
89450 Vézelay
Tel: 03 86 33 23
www.vezelaytourisme.com

The return of the vine

Vines returned to Vézelay in the 1970s thanks to a local councillor who planted two trial hectares at Asquins. The local cooperative, called Henry de Vézelay after a thirteenth-century adviser to the French throne, has been a major force since 1979. It is responsible for half of Vézelay's wine production. Bernard Raveneau (see p.45) was director from 1992–4 during a temporary absence from his family's Chablis estate.

Another important player, as at Joigny (see p.41) is a Michelin-starred restaurateur, in this case Marc Meneau of the restaurant l'Espérance (see box, right).

The wine of Vézelay has quite an upmarket feel, more than one might expect from its legal classification. This is just "Bourgogne Vézelay" and it came into effect (it's for white wines only) in 1997. The whites of Vézelay

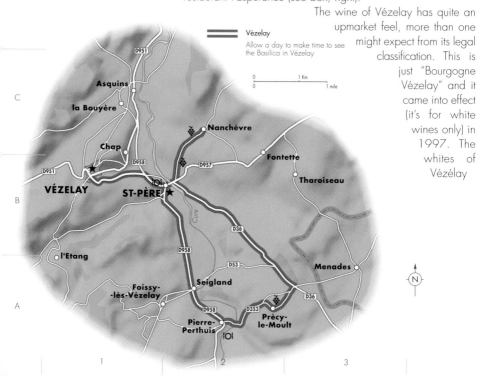

Vézelay

Allow a day to make time to see
the Basilica in Vézelay

are therefore one step up from basic "Bourgogne". The fourteen-strong co-op must be the only one in France to insist on complete hand-harvesting, and a number of its members now work organically. Many wines are just the pleasant but simple kind that come from young vines, and other cooperatives mutter that their Vézelay colleagues are too expensive: I disagree.

ABOVE *'Till recently, this extraordinary place only made ordinary wine.*

The setting
These are the only wines in Burgundy to come from a state-protected beauty spot; Vézelay and the surrounding villages form the northern tip of the 22,530ha of the Parc Naturel Régional du Morvan, legally designated as such in 1970. The Morvan is a region of hill forests, with thin, granite soils that historically meant it was thinly peopled, but home to large populations of bats, foxes, badgers, and wild boar. (The vineyards are on granite pebbly clay and limestone, with innumerable fossils). Vézelay's tourist office (*see* left) has advice on footpaths, horse-riding, bike hire, and so on.

Visiting Vézelay
There are various wine shops, including a joint enterprise run by the Yonne's three cooperatives of Chablis, Bailly, and Vézelay (Les Caves du Pèlerin, *see* box opposite). But I'd recommend concentrating on the main attraction: the luminous Romanesque basilica of Mary Magdalen. This was a staging post for pilgrims setting off on the 1,500km (950-mile) journey to the shrine of St James at Compostela in northwestern Spain.

St Bernard of Clairvaux, the founder of the Cistercian order, preached the second crusade here in 1146, and it was the starting point for the third crusade, led by Richard the Lionheart and the French king Philip II Augustus.

Less than 2km (1.2 miles) away in St-Père, the tracery of the village church of Nôtre Dame makes stone look weightless; a late Gothic achievement that almost compares with the early medieval magnificence of Vézelay.

Where to stay
At l'Espérance, if you can afford it. Otherwise, a room amid the formal French gardens of the superior *chambres d'hôte* of Val en Sel (1 chemin de la Fontaine 89450, St-Père-sous-Vézelay, tel: 03 86 33 26 95). Or in Pierre-Perthuis, with its dramatic high and low level bridges over the river Cure, try the Hôtel-Restaurant Les Deux Ponts (tel: 03 86 32 31 31). Elise Villiers herself (*see* above) offers *gîte* accommodation. For a full list apply to the Vézelay Office de Tourisme (*see* left).

GROWERS IN VEZELAY

Domaine Elise Villiers
Précy-le-Moult
89450 Pierre-Perthuis
Tel: 03 86 33 27 62 *(A3)*
An exceptionally conscientious grower, harvesting her small (5ha) holding by hand and avoiding chemical sprays. Four-fifths Chardonnay, one-fifth Pinot Noir. Lively, minerally wines.

Cave Henri de Vézelay
route de Nanchèvres
89450 St-Père
Tel: 03 86 33 29 62 *(C2)*
Pure-tasting wines, many now organic. The curiosity is the Melon de Bourgogne grape, which is called Muscadet near Nantes in the Loire. This is a much gentler, rounder wine than Muscadet.

**Marc Meneau
L'Espérance**
route de Vézelay
89450 St-Père-sous-Vézelay
Tel: 03 86 33 39 10 *(B2)*
The cellar is next to the fabulous restaurant.

PRICES: inexpensive

The northern Côte de Nuits: Dijon to Vougeot

If you drive here from Paris, there's an hour-long interval of granite hills after the Yonne vineyards of Chablis – and then suddenly you're among some of the most famous wine names in the world. Sightseeing may seem a more affordable option here than actually buying wine – yet there are bargains, even within striking distance of the famed Clos de Vougeot and Le Chambertin.

What is the Côte d'Or?

The vineyards of the Côte d'Or are on east-facing, rising ground. These aren't dramatic hill vineyards, like the riverside slopes of the Douro – the land of Port – or even the northern Rhône's Côte-Rôtie. But there's something satisfying about this 55km (34-mile) ribbon of vines. It's partly to do with the succession of great villages, often alternating between supposedly "masculine" and "feminine" wines, partly the ease of understanding the lie of the land – the best vineyards are midway up the slope – and partly just the look of the place, particularly in the golden month of October.

BELOW *The Côte d'Or not only supplied Dijon with wines, but with the limestone for its handsome buildings.*

Technically, the Côte d'Or is a long tear in the earth's crust where it buckled and split around twenty-five million years ago – during the Cenozoic era, the so-called "age of the mammals".

The north-south rift opened up previous east-west cracks, exposing limestone layers laid down in different eras, and creating a mix of soils that's complex on the slopes, but becomes homogeneous when you get down to the clays and sands of the plain of the river Saône. The result is a great diversity of vineyard soils, creating differences in the wines that you don't need much expertise to be able to appreciate.

Travelling around

For much of the Côte de Nuits, you only really need to make one decision: whether to move from place to place relatively quickly on the N74, or to pootle more slowly down the little D122 as far as Vougeot. Either way there's plenty to see.

Between two presses

This chapter covers the north of the Côte de Nuits, a section of the strip that sits between two historic press houses: that of the dukes of Burgundy at Chenôve in the north, and the Clos de Vougeot in the south. During the heyday of the duchy of Burgundy (1363–1477) the Clos du Roi and Clos du Chapitre at Chenôve were famous vineyard names. Today Chenôve is swallowed up in the appellation of Marsannay, which itself was only recognised in its own right as late as 1987.

So why has the Côte Dijonnaise, the vineyards nearest to Burgundy's capital, Dijon, fallen into relative obscurity? One reason was that a large local market demanded quantity rather than quality, and this was met by planting Gamay, not Pinot. When vineyards from the south of France began to compete, the local wine industry withered. There are still scattered holdings on the north side of Dijon's river, the Ouche, near the village of Daix. On the southern outskirts new building has encroached on the Chenôve vineyards, despite their glorious history. Cities and vineyards find it hard to co-exist: even the *premier cru* sites near Beaune don't have quite the lustre they deserve.

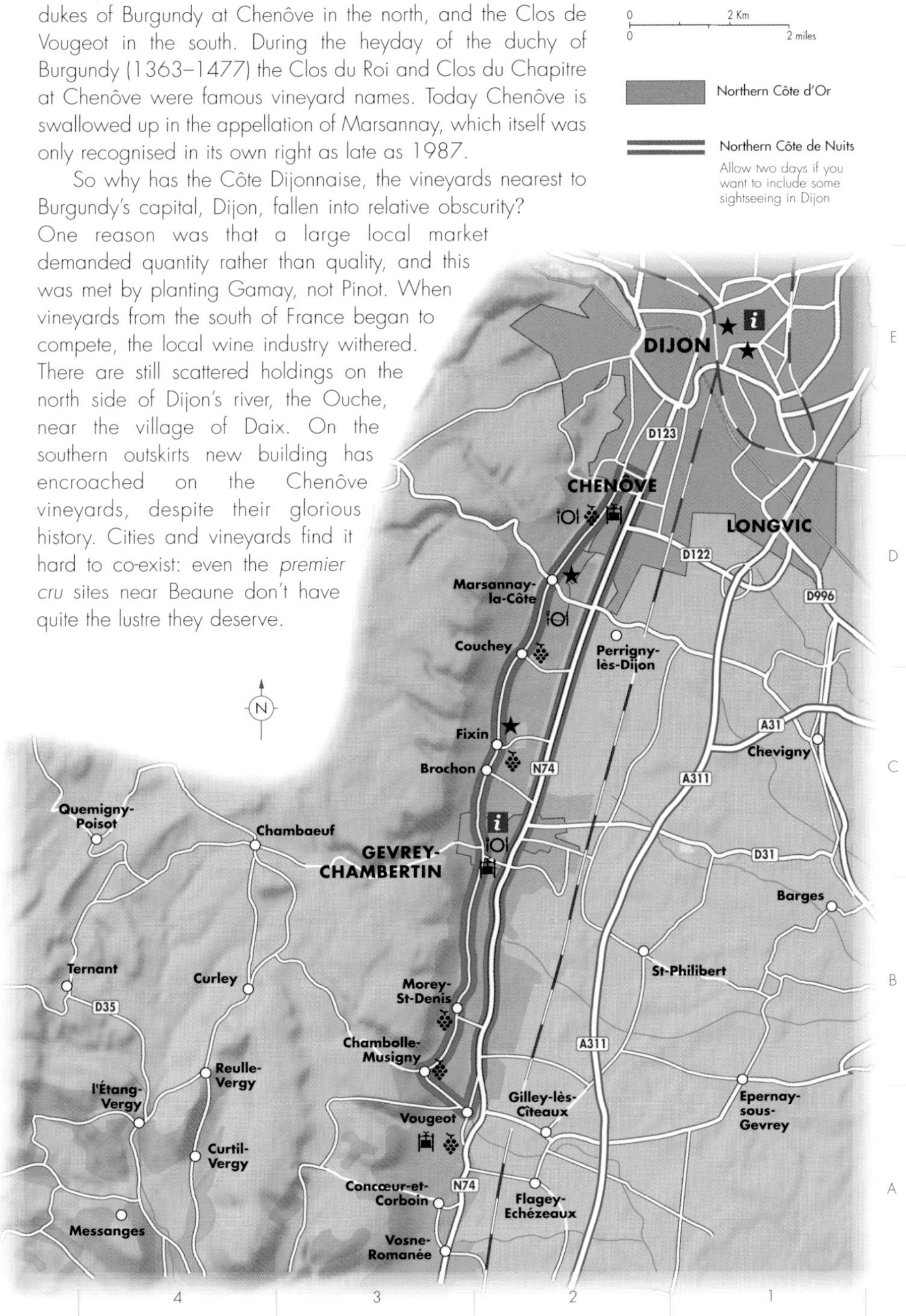

| 0 | | 2 Km |
| 0 | | 2 miles |

Northern Côte d'Or

Northern Côte de Nuits

Allow two days if you want to include some sightseeing in Dijon

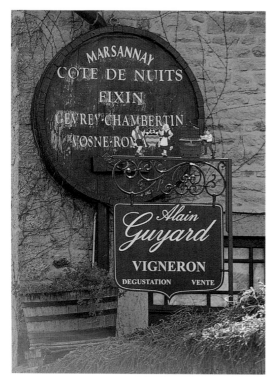

ABOVE *Many growers offer a range of appellations, from simple to world-famous.*

RIGHT *Burgundy's most famous estate, the Domaine de la Romanée-Conti in Vosne, is typically unassuming-looking.*

Dijon for wine lovers

Burgundy's capital is not a centre of the wine trade. It has its Fêtes de la Vigne on the first Sunday in September, but this is more an international folk music festival than a real part of the wine calendar.

But you can't understand Burgundy without having a feel for its glorious and independent past. Dijon's identity went on developing long after it became part of France in 1477, and its eighteenth-century streets have the grandeur of a major provincial capital. It's also an important university town. Much of the ducal palace was built long after the rule of the Valois dukes, but within it you can find some important survivals from that glorious era. The Musée des Beaux-Arts (tel: 03 80 74 52 70) forms part of the Palais des Etats in the ducal palace in the rue des Forges. Start with the ducal kitchens, whose soaring interiors give an impression of the central role of food and wine in the fifteenth century. The highpoint is the banqueting room built by duke Philippe III "Le Bon"(1419–67). This room, known since the seventeenth century as the Salle des Gardes, now houses the tombs of the dukes, which until the revolution lay in Dijon's Carthusian monastery, the Chartreuse de Champmol. Among the high gothic masterpieces are the tombs of Philippe le Hardi (1363–1404) and Jean-sans-Peur (1404–19).

Dijon mustard

Dijon mustard, which you find in almost every decent supermarket throughout the world, does not legally have to come from Dijon. But it wouldn't have existed without these vineyards. Mustard's piquancy comes from mixing the crushed seeds, with *verjus* in the case of Dijon mustard; *verjus* is the sour juice of unfermented and unripe grapes, which was widely used instead of vinegar during the middle ages. Many northern vineyards made *verjus* in years when a poor summer did not allow winemaking because the grapes were not ripe enough. In 1752 Jean Naigeon of Dijon substituted *verjus* for vinegar, and created Moutarde de Dijon. For an in-depth exploration, take the hour-long guided tour at the Musée de la Moutarde, (8 quai Nicolas Rolin, tel: 03 80 44 11 44).

A visit to Chenôve

The press-house of the Dukes of Burgundy is at 8 rue Roger Salengro (tel: 03 80 51 55 00). These two 600-year-old wine presses once turned the harvest of the ducal estate at Chenôve into wine, and their huge size reveals the scale of that operation. This estate, first mentioned in 1228, stretched over around 50ha: the same size as its monastic counterpart the Clos de Vougeot 13km (8 miles) to the south. But whereas Vougeot today has 200 inhabitants Chenôve is a New Town of more than 26,000 – and its vineyard has shrunk to less than 30ha. The presses continued working until 1926. On the third weekend of September they come back into use as part of a celebration called the Reveil des Pressoirs; the "reawakening of the presses".

A good grower to visit in this area is Véronique Tissier (7 impasse Henri Marc, tel: 03 80 51 90 77). Véronique has 3ha of vines, with a rarity: some Pinot Gris. She sells by the bottle; some neighbours also buy her wine by the barrel.

The restaurant, Le Clos du Roy (35 avenue 14 Juillet, 21300 Chenôve, tel: 03 80 54 04 04 for reservations), is geared up for tourists but completely authentic – a common French combination.

Marsannay-la-Côte

Why the long hyphenated name? It's almost the exception in the Côte d'Or to find a village with an unhyphenated name. Marsannay was one of the first to tag on a second descriptor, in 1783, in this case to identify it with the wine villages to the south rather than with Dijon. Marsannay growers are confident that certain of their vineyards will soon be classed as *premier*

GROWERS IN MARSANNAY

Domaine Charles Audoin
7 rue de la Boulotte
21160 Marsannay-la-Côte
Tel: 03 80 52 34 24 (*D2*)
Audouin gets deeper colours than some of his neighbours.

Domaine Bruno Clair
5 rue du Vieux Collège
21160 Marsannay-La-Côte
Tel: 03 80 52 28 95 (*D2*)
Marsannay's major player, *le moteur* ("the motor") of the appellation.

Domaine Fougeray de Beauclair
44 rue Mazy
21160 Marsannay-la-Côte
Tel: 03 80 52 21 12 (*D2*)
Very good and well-priced. There's a 100 per cent Pinot Blanc white burgundy.

Olivier Guyot
39 rue de Mazy
21160 Marsannay-la-Côte
Tel: 03 80 52 39 71 (*D2*)
This small domaine has gone back to horse-ploughing. It chooses not to announce its organic status on the label.

Domaine Huguenot Père et Fils
7 ruelle du Carron
21160 Marsannay-la-Côte
Tel: 03 80 52 11 56 (*D2*)
These wines get some of their interest from properly mature vineyards.

PRICES: moderate to expensive, the latter if from a potential *premier cru*

cru. The same pushiness got this village its own appellation in 1987 – before that it just made generic Bourgogne. The spirit of enterprise dates back at least to 1919 when Joseph Clair returned from World War I and created something unique in the Côte d'Or: a Pinot Noir rosé. His grandson Bruno insists that this requires to be kept for at least a year before drinking. Rosé can be thought of as a red wine vinified like a white wine, and so rosé can play to Pinot Noir's strengths: fine aromas rather than colour or structure. Even Marsannay's red wines tend to be light; in the gender classification, this village is a girl.

A visit to Marsannay
Stop in at the local museum, Maison du Patrimonie et du Tourisme (41 rue de Mazy, tel: 03 80 52 27 73). There's a display respresenting the daily life of growers in the late nineteenth century, with costumes, tools and so on. It's for those, like me, who like small-town museums. (You can visit the website www.ot-marsannay.com for more information.)

A good place to stay is the *chambres d'hôte*, an eighteenth-century farmhouse owned by local wine-growers François and Anne Brugère. You could even try the Michelin-starred restaurant Les Gourmets in Marsannay.

What does "château" mean in Burgundy?
In Marsannay, and often elsewhere in the Côte d'Or, there is a village château; but Burgundy is different to Bordeaux, where virtually all the great estates are called Château this or that.

In Burgundy, the key word is "domaine", and a domaine will usually own vines in a number of separate villages. (By contrast, a Bordeaux château's vineyards are usually all together, and surround the château like a garden.)

So, whereas in Bordeaux it's usual for a property to make one wine, called "Château This" or "Château That", and perhaps a second wine with a different name, a Burgundian domaine will make a dozen wines or more from half a dozen different villages. Each wine will be labelled with its village and/or its vineyard name.

A château in Burgundy will be the local grand house. It may or may not have vineyards attached. Sometimes it will, as in Marsannay, be owned by a big négociant firm (in this case Patriarche) as a tourist attraction, with potential for corporate hospitality. The nearest Burgundy has to the Bordeaux château is the concept of the "monopole", where a whole vineyard has just one owner. There are not all that many of these.

Fixin
Fixin (pronounced "Fissin"), the next village south, is a much smaller place than Marsannay, but produces bigger, beefier

wine – though similarly quite keenly priced. This attractive little village also houses one of Burgundy's most oddly conceived sculptural projects.

Captain Claude Noisot served for seven years in Napoleon's Imperial Guard in Russia, in exile on Elba and at Waterloo. His last wish, unfulfilled due to the rockiness of Fixin's soil, was to be buried upright, sword drawn, in front of the statue he commissioned in 1845 from the sculptor François Rude, showing "Napoleon awakening to immortality". Less reverent critics have suggested that the Emperor looks more like a visitor to a pop festival whose tent has been stolen in the night. Behind the statue in the centre of Fixin are a park and small museum which also commemorate the great man.

A visit to Fixin

Domaine Pierre Gelin is the main producer in Fixin, and the one who owns the inevitably named *premier cru* Clos Napoléon as a *monopole* (*see* above). My favourite growers in Fixin, though are Vincent and Denis Berthaut. They offer a good example of the excellent-value appellation Côte du Nuits-Villages, from the next village south, Brochon.

From Fixin a short walk back up the D122 brings you to the hamlet of Fixey where the church of St Antony (closed on weekdays, tel 03 80 52 45 52) dates from 902AD and is the oldest on the Côte d'Or.

GROWERS IN FIXIN

Domaine Pierre Gelin
2 rue de Chapitre
21220 Fixin
Tel: 03 80 52045024 *(C3)*

Vincent and Denis Berthaut
9 rue Noisot
21220 Fixin
Tel: 03 80 52 45 48 *(C3)*
PRICES: expensive

BELOW *As Dijon grew, so its vineyards shrank.*

GROWERS IN GEVREY

Pierre Bourrée
13 route de Beaune
21220 Gevrey-Chambertin
03 80 34 30 25
To sample an opposite
approach to red burgundy
(see Bouvier, below), try
the old-fashioned style
of this small négociant.

Domaine René Bouvier
29 bis route de Dijon
21220 Gevrey-Chambertin
Tel: 03 80 52 21 37 (C2/3)
Bernard Bouvier has moved
operations down from
the family village of
Marsannay; this is quite
a large estate (17ha) with
holdings all the way up to
Dijon, where the family own
the rudely named Montre-
Cul vineyard. Quite soft,
deep Marsannay, sometimes
low in acidity for my taste.
Many bargains.

**Domaine Philippe
Charlopin-Parizot**
18 route de Dijon
21220 Gevrey-Chambertin
Tel: 03 80 51 81 18 (C2/3)
This grower, who has also
moved between Marsannay
and Gevrey, is a disciple of
the great Henri Jayer (see
p.67), using the master's
signature techniques of
removing the grapes from
their skins and letting them
soak on their skins before
starting fermentation.
He has wines from less
expensive Fixin and simple
Bourgogne Rouge.

**Domaine Michel et Sylvie
Esmonin**
1 rue Neuve
21220 Gevrey-Chambertin
Tel: 03 80 34 37 25 (C2/3)
Elegant wines and a range
that includes less expensive
appellations.

PRICES: expensive

Brochon

This village appears to have been punished for its history of making bulk wine for the Dijon market by being restricted to the generic appellation Côte de Nuits-Villages, which it shares with a number of villages at the southern end of the Côte de Nuits (see p.66). Visitors mainly go to see its château, built in 1900 in almost Disneyesque homage to the sixteenth-century châteaux of the Loire.

Some of the best examples of the village's wine are made by Berthaut in Fixin, Fougeray de Beauclair in Marsannay, and by René Bouvier in Gevrey-Chambertin.

Gevrey-Chambertin

Great success can have a kind of deadening effect on wine villages, and Gevrey-Chambertin – which is one of the most famous in the world – is a case in point. On the positive side you enjoy being in a place where some world-famous wine is grown or made, and it's a starting point for a spectacular hike up the Côte. There are great restaurants – and even a few affordable wines to buy.

Just looking...

The most important name in this village is surely the Domaine Armand Rousseau (1 rue de l'Aumônerie). This is the estate that put domaine-bottled burgundy in the map in the 1930s. But as usual in Burgundy, Armand's son and grandson live in an entirely unpretentious house, and as is usual at their level of celebrity, are not open for visits.

A newer star is Denis Mortet (22 rue de l'Eglise). Again, don't bother knocking or telephoning. However, you can visit the satisfyingly sturdy early medieval Château de Gevrey-Chambertin (tel: 03 80 34 36 13) that overlooks the village – the wine here is made by the owners – the okay but not especially exciting négociant house of Labouré Roi.

Bertin's field

But you will want to see Chambertin – possibly the world's most famous single vineyard, at least for red wine – which lies a short walk out of the village along the D122 south in the direction of Morey-St-Denis.

Napoleon apparently insisted that this wine went with him on all his campaigns, and its reputation led the villagers in 1847 to petition Louis-Philippe, the so-called "citizen-king", to rechristen what had previously been plain Gevrey. Unlike other famous Burgundy vineyards this was not originally a walled monastic clos, but the vineyard that a farmer called Bertin planted next to the longer-established clos named after the abbey of Bèze, northeast of Dijon.

The wrong side of the road

Gevrey is famous for its *grand cru* vineyards – there are eleven, including Chambertin itself. But it's also unusual for having a large amount of village-appellation land on the east side of Route Nationale 74, which in most communes would be inexpensively classed as plain Bourgogne Rouge.

The reason is that the soils here are not the usual clay and sand but pebbles and debris washed down from the *combe Lavaux*, the valley above Gevrey.

But, while there's a lot of village-level-quality Gevrey made, it's not always worth the prices that accrue from its proximity to Chambertin.

A view of the Alps

The same valley that created Gevrey's unique geology also offers some of the sheerest slopes on the Côte. It's a magnet for hill-walkers, and even mountain-climbers.

One lure is the view: if you get right to the top, you can, on a very clear day, see Mont Blanc in the French Alps. Follow the D31 east through the vineyards (if you are in a car leave it at the car park of La Combe Lavaux, beside a crossroads).

Carry on by foot until you see a footpath on the right, initially marked with a yellow-coded sign (these mark the hill routes between Dijon and Nuits-St-Georges).

You want to follow the blue signs, which mark the Sentier des Crêtes (the "crest path") which will lead you on a stiff 8km (5-mile) hike around the valley.

Where to stay and eat in Gevrey-Chambertin

Try Aux Vendanges de Bourgogne. It's a nice old hotel with a good restaurant too, and it's a fine place to get to know the local growers' wine (*see* p.64).

If you can afford it, because it's fairly expensive, a great place to eat has to be the restaurant Les Millésimes. More realistically, try the Bonbistrot, part of the pricey La Rotisserie du Chambertin, or pay a visit to La Sommelerie. (*See* p.64.)

BELOW *Natural exuberance: bolster your energies in Dijon for a 20km (12-mile) hike to Nuits-Saint-Georges via the bridle path along the slopes of the Côte.*

Morey-St-Denis and Chambolle-Musigny

Of these two small neighbouring villages, Chambolle, at the bottom of a wooded valley with a little river, the Grône, is especially pretty.

Morey did not add a vineyard name to its own until the mid-1920s partly because of endless arguments over which of several formerly Cistercian *grand cru* vineyards to tag on. Clos la Roche is the most famous one, but Morey-la-Roche wasn't felt to sound as good as the final choice. The other *grands crus* here are Bonnes-Mares, Clos-des-Lambrays and Clos de Tart.

Growers to visit in Morey-St-Denis and Chambolle-Musigny

There are few real bargains here, but I'd be tempted to visit one of my favourite expensive producers, the Domaine des Lambrays, which owns the *clos* of the same name *en monopole* (rue Basse, 21220 Morey-St-Denis, tel: 03 80 51 84 33). The cheapest wine is the Morey village appellation, and that is €26 a bottle, I'm afraid. On the other hand, Jean-Paul Magnien has some pretty interesting old-vine Bourgogne, from vineyards just across the Route Nationale, for under €9 (5 ruelle de l'Eglise, 21220 Morey-St-Denis).

Chambolle-Musigny is a little over 1km (0.7 miles) away and you might want to park in Morey and walk there along the back road, the D122. The attractions of the village include a good restaurant, Le Chambolle Musigny (tel: 03 80 62 86 26) and the wall paintings, dating from 1530, in the choir of the village church. The drawback is that it would be a pity to miss the chance of buying some of Ghislaine Barthod's Bourgogne Rouge – a wine with a humble appellation but an international following. Ghislaine and her wines epitomise Chambolle's qualities of grace, perfume and delicacy (rue du Lavoir, tel: 03 80 62 80 16) .

Vougeot

Not all Burgundy's great vineyards look the part. However the 50ha Clos de Vougeot is an impressive sight, enclosed by monastic walls and dominated by the Cistercians' sixteenth-century château (Château du Clos de Vougeot, tel: 03 80 62 86 09.)

This is also the headquarters of the robed Confrérie des Chevaliers du Tastevin, whose costumes and rituals date all the way back to… the 1930s. The genesis of the Clos de Vougeot lay in a small gift of land to the monastery of Cîteaux in 1110, but it took its present form in 1336 when the monks enclosed the estate, which had grown to its present size as a result of further gifts and land-swaps. The monks built a press-house and cellar in the austere style of their order, then in 1551 Dom

Losier, the forty-eighth abbot, built the present, still quite plain château as a centre for hospitality. After the revolution and dissolution of the monasteries the Clos remained in the hands of different single owners until 1860 when it was divided. There are now more than fifty separate owners.

Why are people sniffy about the wine?

At only two other points in the whole of the Côte does a *grand cru* vineyard extend so far down the slope – the Route Nationale runs along its eastern wall. So critics argue that some of the lower-lying vines would be better classified as *premier cru*, or even as village wine.

But you are safe in the hands of the best growers: Méo-Camuzet from Vosne-Romanée (*see* p.69), François Faiveley from Nuits-St-Georges (*see* p.67) or Domaine Leroy, based in Auxey-Duresses (*see* p.88).

The Chevaliers du Tastevin

To me, Burgundy's costumed *confréries* have all the glamour and authenticity of a bespectacled man in a town crier's costume bawling "Oyez! Oyez!". But it's a matter of taste, and the aims of the Chevaliers – to defend authentic wines and make them better known – are laudable. It is loosely based on the knightly order of the Golden Fleece, the Toison d'Or, instituted by Duke Philippe III "Le Bon" in 1430.

Growers to visit in Vougeot

The best bet is to plan a *rendez-vous* at Domaine Bertagna, owned by an Anglo-German couple, where the wine is made by local girl Claire Forrestier. Forrestier learned her trade at top estates in the south of France and California before coming here to Domaine Bertagna. It makes a rarity: a white Vougeot *premier cru*, but for many the main attraction will be the inexpensive Hautes-Côtes de Nuits (rue du Vieux Château, 21640 Vougeot, tel: 03 80 62 86 04).

If you want to stay in Vougeot, Domaine Bertagna owns the good and not too expensive Hôtel de Vougeot (18 rue du Vieux Château, tel: 03 80 62 01 15) which is just a few paces from the domaine.

LEFT *Haunting: the scent of vine flowers in spring.*

BELOW *Haunting: Napoleon awakens from the dead in the Parc Noisot, Fixin.*

The southern Côte de Nuits:
Côtes de Nuits-Villages and the
Hautes-Côtes de Nuits

A s you drive south from Vougeot the great wine names continue with Nuits-St-Georges. But launch yourself up one of the valleys and suddenly everything changes. The air is fresher, the roads wind and climb between barely inhabited villages; you still find vineyards, but they too look different, and are scattered among woods, fields of soft fruit, and orchards. The Hautes-Côtes, fancifully called "The Burgundian Alps", look magical, and the wines have a reputation – not always earned – for value for money.

BELOW lyre-trained vines in spring. The new growth will be split between the two arms of the V-shaped trellis.

Travelling around (*see* map p.68)

If the last chapter's route was a succession of wine villages, this itinerary is an exercise in contrasts. We start with the most classic Côte de Nuits communes: Nuits-St-Georges, then Vosne-Romanée, via a detour to nearby Flagey-Echézeaux. These are awesome wines, generally not for sale, and there isn't much to see. So, from Vosne we climb into the Hautes-Côtes de Nuits: Villars-Fontaine, with a detour up to Reulle-Vergy, then back to Marey-lès-Fussey and Magny-lès-Villers.

Then down to the Route Nationale again, and the little-visited Côte des Pierres. Like the Hautes-Côtes, the villages of Corgoloin and Comblanchien make affordable red wines but in a more chewy and serious style. Corgoloin marks the frontier with the Côtes de Beaune – but we finish by going back to Nuits-St-Georges on the RN74 through Prémeaux-Prissey.

Nuits-St-Georges

Nuits, which added the vineyard name of St-Georges in 1892, is Burgundy's second wine town after Beaune. There's a charity auction in the spring, and it's the base for several négociant houses. It has suffered rather from the demolition of its medieval walls. Whereas, Beaune is tucked behind fortifications, the traffic grinds through Nuits-St-Georges along the RN74. The compensation is that this place feels like a working town, not a tourist trap.

Nuits also seems to attract the innovators of the wine business. In the 1980s the man in the news was Nuits-based consultant Guy Accad, with his avoidance of chemicals in the vineyard, and controversial advocacy of ultra-long, ultra-cold macerations of crushed red grapes. Today's pioneers include Nicolas Potel, a new-wave négociant, and Dominique Laurent, a former patissier turned négociant, advocate of lots and lots of new oak. Potel has some interesting stuff in affordable appellations, including the Beaujolais *crus* (*see* p.121).

The legends make some cheaper wine – but not much

I was astonished when I discovered that Henri Jayer of Vosne-Romanée, one of the most celebrated growers in Burgundy, makes some simple Bourgogne Rouge – the cheapest appellation. It was like discovering that Michelangelo had been a part-time jobbing house-painter. But many estates have some vineyards on the "wrong" side of the N74.

On the one hand it's an excuse to go into some legendary cellars, taste, and buy inexpensive wine (basic Burgundy isn't much more than €10 a bottle). But the cheapest wine is often only available in the autumn. Check first and don't overdo this gambit when visiting cellars.

Sightseeing

Nuits-St-Georges has a classic small-town museum with Gallo-Roman findings, and also military mementoes of the Franco-Prussian war of 1870 (12 rue Camille-Rodier, tel: 03 80 62 01 37). There is also the superbly named Cassissium (Impasse des Frères Montgolfier, tel: 03 80 62 49 70, www.cassissium.com), a short drive out of town in the direction of the motorway, with everything you could want to know about cassis, Burgundy's other alcoholic drink. The thirteenth-century church, St-Symphorien, is currently undergoing restoration. (The tourist office is at 3 rue Sonoys, tel: 03 80 62 11 17, www.ot-nuits-st-georges.fr).

From Flagey-Echézeaux to Vosne-Romanée

There's no special reason to meander across the flatlands to the nondescript village of Flagey-Echézeaux. But, one great winemaker lives here (*see* right) and there's a good restaurant (for details *see* restaurant box, p.72).

In Vosne-Romanée, stroll up to 1 rue Derrière la Four and inspect the estate buildings of Burgundy's most famous estate, Domaine de la Romanée-Conti, before taking a look at the world's most famous vineyard, La Romanée-Conti. You can't buy any wine here – you can only buy through the trade – but the co-owners, Aubert and Pamela de Villaine, own another

GROWERS IN NUITS-ST-GEORGES

Domaine Jean Chauvenet
3 rue de Gilly
21700 Nuits-St-Georges
Tel: 03 80 61 00 72 (**C4**)
Quite a lot of inexpensive and reliable Côtes de Nuits-Villages.

Domaine Chauvenet-Chopin
97 rue Félix Tisserand
21700 Nuits-St-Georges
Tel: 03 80 61 00 72 (**C4**)
Perhaps my top choice in Nuits-St-Georges.

Maison Joseph Faiveley
8 rue du Tribourg
21700 Nuits-St-Georges
Tel: 03 80 61 04 55 (**C4**)
Not geared up for visits.

Maison Dominique Laurent
2 rue Jaques Duret
21700 Nuits-St-Georges
Tel: 03 80 61 49 94 (**C4**)
See main text.

Domaine Chantal Lescure
34 A rue Thurot
21700 Nuits-St-Georges
Tel: 03 80 61 16 79 (**C4**)
www.domaine-lescure.com
Look here for red and white village Nuits-St-Georges and red and white Côtes de Beaune.

Moillard-Grivot
rue Caumont Bréon
21700 Nuits-St-Georges
Tel: 03 80 62 42 10 (**C4**)
And separate shop:
Le Caveau de la Berchère
route de Dijon
Tel: 03 80 62 42 48

Maison Nicolas Potel
44 rue des Blés
21700 Nuits-St-Georges
Tel: 03 80 62 15 45 (**C4**)
See main text.

PRICES: expensive

excellent estate 44km (27 miles) away in the Côte Chalonnaise (*see* p.101).

The tiny D109 leads up into the Hautes-Côtes de Nuits from Vosne; the first village you encounter is Concoeur-et-Corboin. When following our itinerary, the turn onto the D35 for Villars-Fontaine is a very sharp one.

Something funny about those vines

Up in the Hautes-Côtes you see scattered vineyards rather than the sea of vines that's become familiar. They will be the same grape varieties, but planted in broadly-spaced rows 3m (10 feet) rather than 1m (3 feet) apart. These mean that the farmers can use conventional tractors rather than the specialized (and expensive, and rather dangerous) *tracteurs enjambeurs* that straddle the rows on long legs.

With wide rows farmers can't plant as densely. The old-fashioned vineyards, designed originally to be horse-ploughed, have around 10,000 vines per hectare. The maximum with conventional tractors is around 4,000. In compensation the individual vines are allowed to grow twice as high. The idea for these so-called *vignes hautes* or

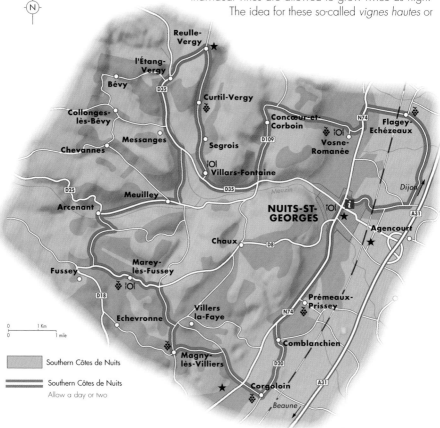

vignes larges was imported from the Entre-Deux-Mers region of Bordeaux in the 1970s, which in turn had copied them from the big Austrian producer Lenz Moser. The reason they haven't been accepted in the top appellations is that the system requires each vine to crop more heavily – and low cropping is (rightly) considered the key to great wine. Close planting also makes the vines create deep roots to explore every geological nuance of the soil.

A third system is popular with some Burgundy producers: *vignes en lyre*, the lyre system of training, in which the vines' leafy branches are formed into two splayed walls of vegetation. The aim is maximum exposure to air and sunlight, and the system allows the creation of a grassy sward between the rows. The vine density is greater than with *vignes hautes*.

A stop in Villars-Fontaine

This tiny village's restaurant, L'Auberge du Côteau, has an enthusiastic following for its grills, home-made terrines and *fondue bourguignonne* (not cheese, but pieces of Charolais beef cooked at the table). It's cheap – there's a €10 lunch menu – and with the Maison des Hautes-Côtes currently closed (*see* below), it's a good place to try different Hautes-Côtes producers' wines. (It is located at route Départementale 35, 21700 Villars Fontaine, tel: 03 80 61 10 50 for reservations.)

Winemaking in Villars-Fontaine is dominated by the Hudelot family. The brothers Bernard and Henri started their domaine here in 1973, twelve years after the Hautes-Côtes appellation was created. They've now gone their separate ways and are following different philosophies. Henri's son Patrick went officially organic in 2000 (route de Segrois, tel: 03 80 61 50 37, www.domaine-patrick-hudelot.com).

Bernard's estate, now largely run by his daughter Armèle, continues to use pesticides if necessary, but the wines are hardly conventional. The Château de Villars-Fontaine (tel: 03 80 62 31 94, www.domainedemontmain.fr) is dedicated to making wines intended to show their best after ten years' ageing, and have a lot of colour and tannin. The red wine is matured in two lots of new oak barrels. It's not the way most growers work in this humble appellation – they concentrate on juicy, value-for-money wines – but one of the pleasures of Burgundy is the untamed individuality of many growers.

A stop in Marey-lès-Fussey

Marey-lès-Fussey used to be a compulsory stop for its Maison des Vins, which presented the area's wines in the setting of a reasonably priced restaurant. But the owner, Bernard Hudelot (*see* above) has at the time of writing closed it down and is looking for someone else to take it on (watch this space).

GROWERS IN THE SOUTHERN COTE DE NUITS

Domaine Georges Mugneret-Gibourg
5 rue des Communes
21700 Vosne-Romanée
Tel: 03 80 61 01 57 (*C3/4*)
Marie-Christine and Marie-Andrée Mugneret make a little Bourgogne Rouge (although "it's not really our speciality", they say) and a village Vosne.

Henri Gouges
7 rue Moulin
21700 Nuits-St-Georges
Tel: 03 80 61 04 40 (*C4*)
A great historic name.

Domaine Anne et François Gros
11 rue des Communes
21700 Vosne-Romanée
Tel: 03 80 61 07 95 (*C3/4*)
Some excelllent Hautes-Côtes de Nuits and Bourgogne Rouge.

Méo-Camuzet
11 rue des Grands Crus
21700 Vosne-Romanée
Tel: 03 80 61 11 05 (*C3/4*)
There's quite a lot of Hautes-Côtes de Nuits Blanc, a bit of Bourgogne Rouge.

Emmanuel Rouget
18 route Gilly lès Citeaux
21640 Flagey-Echézeaux
Tel: 03 80 62 86 61 (*C/D4*)
Rouget is Henri Jayer's nephew and has now taken over his estate.

PRICES: moderate

GROWERS IN THE SOUTHERN COTE DE NUITS CONTINUED

Domaine Chauvenet-Chopin
and **Domaine Jean Chauvenet**, both in Nuits-St-Georges (see p.67) both make excellent Côte de Nuits-Villages.

Domaine Desertaux-Ferrand
133 Grand Rue
21700 Corgoloin (A3)
An unusual Côte de Nuits-Villages white with some Pinot Blanc.

Domaine Gachot-Monot
3 rue de Bretonnières
21700 Corgoloin
Tel: 03 80 62 93 03 (A3)
A hot name. The unfined and unfiltered reds are real earthy, smoky Côte de Nuits at bargain prices.

Domaine des Perdrix (Rodet)
rue de l'Église
21700 Prémeaux-Prissey
Tel: 03 80 62 30 37 (B3)

Domaine Daniel Rion et Fils
Route Nationale 74
21700 Prémeaux-Prissey
Tel: 03 80 62 31 28 (B3)
Patrice's brothers Olivier and Christophe also have a wide range including Côte de Nuits-Villages.

Michelle et Patrice Rion
1 rue de la Maladière
21700 Prémeaux-Prissey
Tel: 03 80 62 32 63 (B3)
This conscientious producer makes a great-value Bourgogne Rouge.

Domaine de la Vougerie (Boisset)
rue de l'Église
21700 Prémeaux-Prissey
Tel: 03 80 21 62 27 (B3)
See main text.

PRICES: inexpensive

Marey is, though, home to one of the area's biggest producers: Daniel Thévenot of Domaine Thévenot Le Brun et Fils. Unlike the Hudelots, the Thévenots machine-harvest (shame) but they're nice people and there are some good-value wines, including an unusual Pinot Beurot (alias Pinot Gris) (tel: 03 80 62 91 64, www.thevenot-le-brun.com).

At Domaine Jayer-Gilles (21700 Magny-les-Villers, tel: 03 80 62 91 79) Robert Jayer and his son Gilles are cousins of the Jayers of Vosne. Like Henri they believe in new oak; unlike him they're often accused of overdoing it. Holdings are in grand cru appellations as well as up in the hills.

From Magny-lès-Villers a 3km (2 mile) drive back down to the N74 brings us to the main frontier towns of the so-called Côte des Pierres.

Curtil-Vergy
Here, 130m (427 feet) above Vosne-Romanée, are the ruins of the Benedictine monastery of the tenth-century St Vivant, whose monks tended and named the vines of the grand cru clos of Romanée-St-Vivant, which lies opposite La Romanée-Conti. This is a good starting point for walks on the well-marked footpaths to L'Etang-Vergey, with its Disney-like nineteenth-century château., then it's just 2km (1.2 miles) on the D116 to tiny Reulle-Vergy, whose castle is a thousand years older, and is in ruins. Reulle also has a Museum of the Arts and Traditions of the Hautes-Côtes (tel: 03 80 61 40 95).

The (only) wine-grower at Curtil-Vergey is also the main hotelier: Domaine du Val de Vergey (21220 Curtil-Vergey, tel: 03 80 61 43 81). The owner, Yves Chaley, who also runs the Hotel Le Manassès (see below), was the subject of a 2002 Channel 4 television documentary called "Grapes of Wrath" over his campaign to topple Curtil-Vergey's mayor in local elections.

It's only recently that the Hautes-Côtes has become better known for wine than for the soft fruits that go into Crème de Cassis, Framboise and the like. Arcenant is the home of the king of this area's licoristes: Jean-Baptiste Joannet

(tel: 03 80 61 12 23). You can also call on Jean-Paul Lalarme, one of the one-time disciples of Guy Accad (*see above*) – though based in Arcenant his wines are all village-appellation Nuits-St-Georges at around €16. Lalarme's son has taken over from Accad, but they continue along the same lines (rue Basse at Arcenant, tel: 03 80 61 28 60).

Are the Côte de Nuits and the Côte de Beaune really different?

The Côte de Nuits and the Côte de Beaune have real differences in their soils. The limestones of the Côte de Nuits are older – about 160–175 million years old (the Middle Jurassic era). This "strata package" goes underground, and south of Corgoloin we are on younger, Upper Jurassic soils, laid down 141–154 million years ago.

But do the different soils account for the different styles of wine, and if so, how? The trouble is that apparently similar soil mixtures turn up in both Côtes. The soil scientist Claude Bourguignon says that the difference between the geological ages of the soils is only slight. "And when you look at the percentage of clay to limestone in each case there's no difference at all," he adds.

But there is, he says, a difference between the types of clay. "The clays of the Côte de Nuits are significantly heavier and better at water retention. So this means that grapes grown

BELOW *Ecologically minded growers in the Hautes-Côtes leave a grassy sward between high-trained vines (the so-called "vignes hautes").*

on them will have a longer ripening period – which of course suits Pinot Noir. In the Côte de Beaune they're less retentive and this is right for Chardonnay, which is an earlier-ripening variety." But he cautions: "It's one theory, one possible explanation – no more than that."

Of course there are (a few) white wines made north of Corgoloin and some very distinguished reds south of Ladoix – Volnay, Pommard, and red Corton. But it's mainly in the Côte de Nuits that burgundy can satisfy those who consider themselves, mainly, red wine drinkers: people

who look for "big" dark full-bodied wines. There is more tannin, more density, more structure, in Côte de Nuits reds.

Côte des Pierres: Corgoloin and Comblanchien

These two villages are not names to conjure with as they are only allowed to use the generic AC of Côte de Nuits-Villages. The major local industry is quarrying, not winemaking. The local pink Comblanchien limestone is tough enough to use as paving, and is used throughout Orly airport in Paris.

Yet again the gender distinctions of the Côte d'Or apply: Corgoloin makes hard, somewhat "masculine" wines, Comblanchien soft, "feminine" ones. Growers with holdings in both villages have the option of blending.

Prémeaux-Prissey

Untypically this village is south of the N74. The wines use the Nuits-St-Georges appellation, and the village is home to the flagship Côte de Nuits estates of two big négociants, Antonin Rodet, based in Mercurey (see p.103), and Burgundy's biggest player, Jean-Claude Boisset. Rodet's Domaine des Perdrix doesn't have a *caveau* for direct sales, but its neighbour in the Rue de l'Eglise, Boisset's Domaine de la Vougerie, does – and there are some affordable wines, made by Vougerie's talented and charismatic Quebequois winemaker Pascal Marchand, who is one of the people turning around the quality and fortunes of this company. Boisset never used to be highly rated by burgundy-lovers, but that is changing fast.

Beaune and its neighbours

D ijon may be the capital of the province called Burgundy, but Beaune is the capital of the Burgundy wine region. It has medieval cellars, ritzy wine shops, expensive restaurants, antique dealers, and wine tourists in droves. So in one sense it is, as you might suppose, a bad place to buy wine. But Beaune is also a wine appellation, and an oddly invisible one. The dark halo of invisibility also seems to spread out to some of the surrounding villages. Pommard is famous, but Savigny-lès-Beaune and Chorey-lès-Beaune, Ladoix-Serrigny, and Pernand-Vergelesses are relatively obscure, even today, and even the great vineyards of the hill of Corton which overlook Beaune are hardly household names.

Why Corton is so great

On Beaune's doorstep is perhaps the oddest *grand cru* site in the whole of Burgundy. This is Corton – the only hill in the whole of the Côte d'Or that you can walk right round, and its crown of woodland makes it visually unmistakeable. It's also unique in being equally celebrated for intense red wines, from the southeast-facing Corton vineyard (the only red *grand cru* in the Côte de Beaune), and for whites from the west-facing Corton Charlemagne (named supposedly because Charlemagne's wife's preferred white wines, because they didn't stain her husband's beard.)

The soils here are Middle Jurassic; they were laid down a few million years before Chablis' Kimmeridgian, also classed as Middle Jurassic. The white wines, especially from Pernand-Vergelesses, southwest of Corton, can be equally minerally, but quite distinct, and often with a trademark aniseed note.

Beaune's local *premier cru* vineyards include the fabulously named Vigne de l'Enfant Jesus (the wine being supposedly as smooth as the infant Christ's skin), and its red wines are on the whole richly flavoured.

The Rhoin

The valleys that cross the Côte d'Or add interest and variety both to the landscape and the wines. Just north of Beaune is the little river Rhoin, which crosses the outskirts of the city after its 15km

LEFT *Palets stacked high await the finished bottles.*

BELOW *Famous names on sale at a wine shop in Place Carnot, Beaune.*

(9-mile) journey down the Vallée d'Orée from the hamlet of Bouilland where it rises. On its way it divides the vineyards of Savigny-lès-Beaune, and in the course of its long history it has washed quantities of limestone rubble into the Saône valley. The result is that Chorey-lès-Beaune, which on a map looks too far onto the plain to make interesting wines, is in fact a good place for bargains.

Exploring the valley of the Rhoin (*see* map p.78)

This exploration of Beaune and Corton is centred round the valley of the Rhoin, with a brief detour up a second valley to Echevronnes and Changey. The route starts in Beaune, then takes us out to Chorey, then to Ladoix-Serrigny, Aloxe-Corton, Pernand-Vergelesses, Echevronne, and Savigny-lès-Beaune, with the option to continue up the valley to Bouilland and the ruins of the abbey of Ste-Marguerite.

Beaune – beautiful if a little dull

Beaune is a late-medieval and renaissance city whose walled centre seems to defy the effects of time. Its buildings include the superlative fifteenth-century Hôtel-Dieu; the narrow streets, squares and courtyards are on a harmonious human scale. Yet there's an absence of exhilaration; life seems to have drained away – even, according to those who know it, in the course of the last few decades. Perhaps it suffers from the stifling effect of too much money – and it's certainly not a place for the young.

The name derives from Belenos, the Celtic sun god, celebrated with bonfires on Beltane, the original May Day. His name, like that of Toutatis, is familiar if you know the Asterix comics. A settlement developed around a shrine, which grew into a city. Beaune became the seat of the dukes of Burgundy, until Philippe Le Hardi, the first Valois duke, moved the capital to Dijon in 1364. Beaune grew rich from the wool trade before it became famous for wine. Its walls, nearly 2km (1 mile) in length, were built from the fourteenth century onwards; as the city lost its strategic importance the fortifications and their cellars were put to use by the new wine shippers. Bouchard Père et Fils, founded in 1731, bought the old Bastion St-Jean, the eastern strongpoint, as its headquarters in 1810.

In the nineteenth century, the city, with its central position on the rail network, became the wine capital not just of Burgundy but of much of central and southern France. Trains would arrive loaded with barrels from the Mediterranean coast, and leave, after a cursory "baptism" – with "burgundy".

General hospital

It's surprising to think that the Hôtel-Dieu, an exuberant gothic masterpiece built by Flemish architects in the mid-fifteenth century to rival its counterpart in Valenciennes, in the Dukes' northern territories in Flanders, was a working hospital as recently as 1971.

The Hospices de Beaune still runs the town's modern general hospital and the income that the Hospices generates – from visitors to the Hôtel-Dieu and from the auction in November of wine from its 58ha estate – gives patients there the latest medical technology, plus free television, among other benefits. The Hôtel-Dieu hosts a press conference before the November auction, among the raised and partitioned beds of the former main ward, called La Grande Salle des Pôvres; the journalists, and various freeloaders, are then entertained to an inevitably sumptuous lunch in the neighbouring Salle St-Nicolas, where the dying were formerly prepared for their last journey. (Hôtel-Dieu, rue de l'Hôtel-Dieu, tel: 03 80 24 45 00 [below, *B2*].)

Catch the Last Judgement

Don't miss the seventeenth-century automaton spit-turner in the reconstructed kitchens, or, on a more elevated level, the nine panels that constitute the "Last Judgement" attributed to Rogier Van der Weyden and painted between 1445 and 1448. This

The town of Beaune
A quaint if quiet centre – except at the time of the historic auction

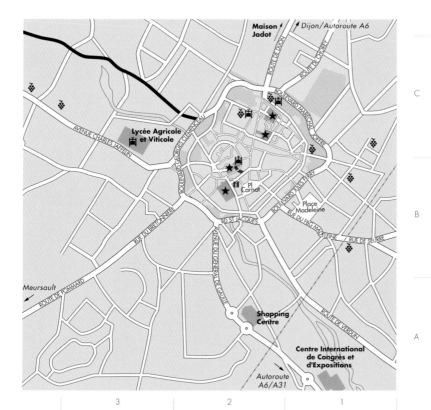

LOCAL INFORMATION

Office de Tourisme
1 rue Hôtel-Dieu
21200 Beaune
Tel: 03 80 26 21 30
www.ot-beaune.fr

Office de Tourisme
13 rue Vauchey Very
21420 Savigny-les-Beaune
Tel: 03 80 26 12 56

great painting was originally the altarpiece of the chapel at the end of the Grande Salle des Pôvres, and patients could be entertained, and chastened, with a glimpse of the hereafter; a bit like television in the ward, but more edifying. On the reverse side is a portrait of Duke Philippe le Bon's wealthy chancellor Nicolas Rolin (c.1376–1462) who founded the Hôtel-Dieu in 1443 and commissioned the painting.

Tour the ramparts, starting either from the Hôtel-Dieu or the Château de Beaune (see p.75, C1), now the Bouchard Père headquarters. Each of the strong points has its own name and history – going clockwise from the Hôtel-Dieu you pass the Bastion Ste-Anne, the Château, then the Bastion Nôtre Dame. Partial demolitions mean you can't do a full circuit.

Buying wine in Beaune

You know you're in a centre of the wine trade from the large number of shops in and around the place Carnot. Some of these offer better value than others. I recommend La Cave des Vielles Vignes (6 bis avenue de la République, tel: 03 80 24 19 44) – one of a chain that claims to offer wines at the grower's cellar-door price. One wine shop is also that particularly French phenomenon, an *espace culturel* with glassware and accessories, but also an excellent wine bookshop: L'Athenaeum de la Vigne et du Vin (7 rue de l'Hôtel-Dieu, tel: 03 80 25 08 30, and check out the website: pro.wanadoo.fr/athenaeum).

BELOW *Visit these cellars, but brace yourself to be underwhelmed by some of the wines*

There's a dedicated wine museum (the Musée du Vin de Bourgogne) to be found in the rue d'Enfer (tel: 03 80 25 08 30) – this is worth a visit if only because it's housed in a sixteenth-century ducal palace.

Beaune is of course the headquarters of the co-ordinating body for the region's growers and négociants, the Bureau Interprofessionel des Vins de Bourgogne. You may not need to visit it (12 boulevard Bretonnière, tel: 03 80 25 04 80) but its website is worth checking out, at www.bivb.com. The BIVB also runs a wine school (6 rue du 16ème Chasseur, tel: 03 80 26 35 11).

But, for perhaps the most revealing look behind the scenes, drop in on the next generation of winemakers at the Lycée Viticole (16 avenue Charles Jaffelin, tel: 03 80 26 35 81) – visits and tastings are by appointment. The wines, incidentally, are very good.

On the beaten track: visiting the négociants

Reine Pédauque is hardly a name to set a wine lover's pulse racing; Patriarche Père et Fils used to be the same, though is now much improved. Both have magnificent and ancient cellars, and both, unlike, say, Louis Jadot (p.78, B3) or Bouchard Père et Fils (p.75, C1), offer well organized guided visits and tastings. (Patriarche: 5–7 rue du Collère, tel: 03 80 24 53 78, www.patriarche.com, p.75, C2; and Caves de la Reine Pédauque: porte St Nicolas, tel: 03 80 22 23 11, www.reine-pedauque.com, p.75, C1/2).

Another good place for a general tasting is a little way out of town. La Cave des Hautes-Côtes on the N74, here called the route de Pommard, (tel: 03 80 25 01 00, p.75, B1) is the Côte d'Or's only growers' cooperative, and has a caveau where there will always be some bottles open for tasting from lots of different appellations.

Off the beaten track: Biodynamic Beaune

Few know that the Beaune appellation is where Burgundy's organic and Biodynamic revolution largely got off the ground. In 1979 Jean-Claude Rateau had just become a grower, having recently left this town's world-famous wine school, where he found himself unconvinced by teachers who argued that agro-chemicals, such as fertilizers, herbicides and pesticides were a force for good in the vineyards.

He read up on organic techniques, as described for example by Sir Alfred Howard (1873-1947), a former agricultural adviser in British-ruled India, and later founder of the Soil Association. During the 1980s he became increasingly convinced by the most rigorous form of organic farming, Biodynamism (La Biodynamie), the doctrines founded on the

GROWERS IN BEAUNE

Maison Alex Gambal
4 rue Jacques Vincent
21200 Beaune
Tel: 03 80 22 75 81 (C1)
A small négociant founded in 1997 by Boston-born Alex Gambal.

Domaine Paul et Emmanuel Giboulot
4 route de Seurre
21200 Beaune
Tel: 03 80 22 90 07 (B1)
See main text.

Maison Camille Giroud
3 rue Pierre-Joigneaux
21200 Beaune
Tel: 03 80 22 12 65 (B1)
This négociant house has long specialized in mature burgundy. Now it's owned by a conglomerate including the cult Napa grower Ann Colgin, and it's managed by American expatriate Becky Wasserman.

Domaine Albert Morot
Château de la Cresotte
2 Avénue Charles Jaffelin
1200 Beaune
Tel: 03 80 22 35 39 (C3)
An excellent producer, but one that has no holdings below the level of premier cru, so there's nothing very cheap here.

Domaine Jean-Claude Rateau
route de Bouze
21220 Beaune
Tel: 03 80 22 52 54 (C4)
See main text.

PRICES: moderate to expensive

GROWERS IN CHOREY-LES-BEAUNE

Arnoux Père et Fils
12 rue Brenots
21200 Chorey-lès-Beaune,
Tel: 03 80 22 57 98 (*B4*)

Château de Chorey-lès-Beaune
21200 Chorey-lès-Beaune
Tel: 03 80 22 06 05 (*B4*)
A bit pricier than most.

Domaine Tollot-Beaut et Fils
21200 Chorey-lès-Beaune
Tel: 03 80 22 16 54 (*B4*)
Fruity, everyday wines.

PRICES: inexpensive

teachings of Rudolph Steiner. His lectures, given in conjunction with the soil scientist Claude Bourguignon, have persuaded most of the region's most famous winemaking names to follow these methods. Jean-Claude Rateau markets his excellent wines in partnership with Beaune's other leading Biodynamic wine producer, Emmanuel Giboulot.

Chorey-lès-Beaune
The flatlands of this little village give a different, more distant view of the Côte. It's a good place to buy cheapish red wine, either with the village appellation (there are no *premier cru* vineyards) or as simple Bourgogne Rouge.

Ladoix-Serrigny
Corgoloin, the frontier village of the Côte de Nuits, is just 4km (2.5 miles) up the road. This northern outpost of the Côte de Beaune is hardly any better known than Corgoloin.

Here, every first Sunday in July, the growers organize a *Balade Gourmande*, or gastro-walk from the neighbouring hamlet of Buisson – five stops on a marked path offer refreshment in the form of village wines and snacks (typically Burgundian things like cheese or terrine or snails) that

Grand cru vineyard

Premier cru vineyard

From Beaune to Savigny
A day trip exploring
Corton and the lesser-
known villages

you can taste on the precise terroir that created them. Ladoix wines, both red and white, are good value. The growers mostly also have holdings in the Corton and Corton-Charlemagne *grands crus*.

Aloxe-Corton

This small village is dominated by big négociants. La Reine Pédauque (*see* p.77) owns the Château de Corton-André, built originally in the fifteenth century, but rebuilt after being destroyed in 1593 in the wars of religion (21420 Aloxe-Corton, tel: 03 80 26 44 25, www.pierre-andre.com).

The château is a landmark with its typically Burgundian multi-coloured roof tiles. You can visit the (original) cellars and taste any day of the week.

Aloxe is also the home of the original estate owned by the négociant house of Louis Latour. This domaine centres on the château based at Corton Grancey, dating from 1749. Latour claims that the fermentation cellars attached to the château, built in 1832, were the first purpose-built winery in France – though I'm not sure where that leaves the Clos de Vougeot or the Pressoir des Ducs de Bourgogne at Chenôve (*see* p.64 and 59 respectively). Domaine Louis Latour is at 21420 Aloxe Corton, tel: 03 80 26 42 63, www.louislatour.com).

The leading estate in Aloxe – Domaine Comte Senard – recently moved its winemaking and offices to Beaune, but in Aloxe you can still find the domaine's *caveau*, to taste and buy (Clos des Meix, 21420 Aloxe-Corton; tel: 03 80 26 41 65, www.domaine senard.com). There's a *table d'hôte* offering a selection of dishes with either four, six or eight wines according to your appetite and your plans for the day, all served and discussed by a sommelier.

GROWERS IN LADOIX-SERRIGNY

Capitain-Gagnerot
38 route de Dijon
21550 Ladoix-Serrigny
Tel: 03 80 26 41 36 (**B6**)
www.capitain-gagnerot.com
Long-established; fought to get the appellation recognised.

Domaine Chevalier Père et Fils
Buisson
21550 Ladoix-Serrigny
Tel: 03 80 26 46 30 (**B6**)
One of the best known Ladoix domaines. Can be a little variable, but some good bottles.

Domaine Edmond Cornu
Le Meix Gobillon
rue du Bief
21550 Ladoix-Serrigny
Tel: 03 80 26 40 79 (**B6**)
Hand-harvested wines, unfined and unfiltered.

Domaine André Nudant
11 Route Nationale 74
21550 Ladoix-Serrigny
Tel: 03 80 26 40 48 (**B6**)
There's good-value village Ladoix and generic Bourgogne here.

Domaine Jean-René Nudant
11 Route Nationale 74
21550 Ladoix-Serrigny
Tel: 03 80 26 40 48 (**B6**)
A range that is usefully weighted towards village wines and simple Bourgogne.

Château de Serrigny/ Domaine Prince Florent de Mérode
rue du Château
21550 Ladoix-Serrigny
Tel: 03 80 26 40 80 (**B6**)
Since 2001 there has been a new and skilful winemaker here.

PRICES: moderate

GROWERS IN ECHEVRONNE
. . . .

Domaine Cornu-Camus
2 rue Varlot
21420 Echevronne
Tel: 03 80 21 57 53 **(D6)**
Here you can taste the difference between the Hautes-Côtes of Nuits and Beaune, which mirror the change of style that takes place on the Côte d'Or itself, from beefier Nuits to smoother Beaune. Fruity wines, enhanced by Pierre Cornu's high fermentation temperatures.

Domaine Lucien Jacob
21420 Echevronne
Tel: 03 80 21 52 15 **(B6)**
One of the estates that campaigned to create the Hautes-Côtes appellation. The wines are good and the estate is a good source of crème de cassis.

PRICES: moderate

BELOW *Vines in the Côte de Beaune sprawl up side valleys, creating a much deeper vineyard strips than in the Côte de Nuits.*

Under a separate estate label, Domaine des Terregelesses, you can find village-level Savigny and Chorey wines.

This estate is part of the recent history of wine in Burgundy, in that Philippe Senard was one of the most enthusiastic followers of the controversial consultant Guy Accad (*see* p.67). On the evidence of the wines today, the estate didn't suffer from the experience.

Jacques Copeau

On your left, as you approach Pernand by the D18, you pass the house where Jacques Copeau, the writer, director, and drama critic, lived from 1925. Copeau was a key figure in the development of modern theatre who believed in liberating it from fussy naturalism and from the early twentieth-century cult of the actor-manager. The inflential intellectual André Gide, winner of the Nobel Prize for Literature in 1947, said there were two schools of theatre – pre- and post-Copeau. Pernand now has a biennial festival of theatre, music, and wine at the end of October (tel: 03 80 21 54 51, www.jacques-copeau.com).

Pernand-Vergelesses

Pernand's stone houses and cellars are bunched on the slopes of a smaller hill beside Corton around a twelfth-century church which, though small, manages to combine a multi-coloured steeple, a Romanesque nave and gothic choir. The streets then lead up through the village, to a view over the vineyards and a nineteenth-century statue of the Madonna.

The great wine name of Pernand is the Domaine Bonneau du Martray (tel: 03 80 21 80 64, but it does not sell direct).

On the main road to Echevronne there's the excellent Rémi Rollin with his large modern cellar (*D5*, tel: 03 80 21 57 31). In the village of Pernand-Vergelesses proper, three names to look out for are Domaine Rapet, its neighbours Regis and Luc Pavelot, and Domaine Jaffelin round the corner in rue du Creux St-Germain.

The village's wines aren't quite the bargains they used to be, but this appellation for me encapsulates what's special about Burgundy – deliciousness, subtlety and the ability to surprise you. From Pernand you can pick up a well-marked footpath up to Echevronne, 4km (2.5 miles) away in the Hautes-Côtes de Beaune (*see* below).

Echevronne

The Hautes-Côtes de Beaune begin at Echevronne – a short drive, or perhaps better still, a walk. The footpath leads on to Changey with its eighteenth-century château, with the option of crossing the valley and returning to Pernand via the Bois de Reure – a route that takes you along part of an ancient highway joining Chalon-sur-Saône with Boulogne and the English Channel. The whole walk is 10 km (6 miles) long.

Savigny-lès-Beaune

Here the wines are – according to a wall inscription of obscure origin – "*nourrisants, théologiques et morbifuges*": "nourishing, doctrinally correct and curative". This endorsement can be read on the wall of the Château de Savigny (dating from 1340, rebuilt in the seventeenth century). There are many other short homilies on the walls of the village, especially in the rue

Chanoine Donin and the rue Guy de Vaulchier, carved between the seventeenth and nineteenth centuries. Like Rully (*see* p.101), Savigny is also a centre for making Crémant de Bourgogne.

Savigny sits across the Vallée d'Orée on the little river Rhoin and is today in the shadow of the A6, the Autoroute du Soleil. The wines are mainly red, and in addition to their alleged virtues are famous for a velvety smoothness – though on the motorway side of the valley the different terroir makes for earthier wines.

Don't miss the vintage car collection in the grounds of the château (tel: 03 80 21 55 03), the Fire Brigades' Museum (15 rue Jacques-Germain, tel: 03 80 21 55 03) or the fifteenth-century wall painting in the village church of St Cassien.

GROWERS IN PERNAND AND SAVIGNY-LES-BEAUNE

Simon Bize et Fils
12 rue Chanoine Donin
21420 Savigny-lès-Beaune
Tel: 03 80 21 50 57 (*D3/4*)
Some of Savigny's most interesting wines.

Lucien Camus-Bruchon
16 rue de Chorey
21420 Savigny-lès-Beaune
Tel: 03 80 26 51 08 (*D3/4*)
Especially good Vieilles Vignes Les Liards.

Domaine Chandon de Briailles
1 rue Soeur-Goby
21420 Savigny-lès-Beaune
Tel: 03 80 21 52 31 (*D3/4*)
The big name here.

Domaine Jaffelin Père et Fils
rue du Creux St-Germain
21420 Pernand-Vergelesses
Tel: 03 80 21 52 43 (*C5*)
See main text.

J-M. et H. Pavelot
1 chemin des Guettottes
21420 Savigny-lès-Beaune
Tel: 03 80 21 55 21 (*D3/4*)
See main text.

Domaine Rapet Père et Fils
rue Paulant
21420 Pernand-Vergelesses
Tel: 03 80 21 57 31 (*C5*)
See main text.

Domaine Regis et Luc Pavelot
rue Paulant
21420 Pernand-Vergelesses
Tel: 03 80 26 13 65 (*C5*)
See main text.

Domaine Rollin Père et Fils
route Echevronne
21420 Pernand-Vergelesses
Tel: 03 80 21 57 31 (*C5*)
See main text.

PRICES: moderate

Bouilland

This former charcoal-burners' settlement is a 10km (6 mile) drive or cycle ride up the Rhoin Valley on the D2. Off to the left are the Romanesque and gothic ruins of the Augustinian abbey of Ste Marguerite, founded, according to local legend, on a site where a local beauty of that name was rescued from the brutal attentions of an armed knight by the miraculous creation of an opening in the rock through which her would-be assailant could not pass. This unusual natural feature can still be seen on the well-marked footpath leading from Bouilland to the abbey.

Where to stay in Beaune and its surroundings

In Beaune itself there's the Hôtel des Remparts (see p.75, B1) which isn't expensive for a central, three-star hotel, or the Hôtel Central (see p.75, B/C 2), a good mid-priced hotel-restaurant in a sixteenth-century house very near the Hôtel-Dieu.

A 3km (1.9-mile) drive from the centre brings you to Chorey-lès-Beaune (see map p.78, A4), with its quirky-looking château, a medieval-renaissance hybrid. There are five guest rooms (www.chateau-de-chorey-les-beaune.fr; see box, p.78).

Only a little further out Aloxe-Corton offers the country-house-hotel experience at the Villa Louise. Expect to pay around €100 a night in the high season. In Savigny, there's the mid-priced and convenient Hôtel L'Ouvrée. In Bouilland there's the luxurious Hostellerie du Vieux Moulin.

For gîtes and chambres d'hôte try the tourist office in Beaune (see box, p.76), or www.tites-de-france-cotedor.com; the latter covers the whole département.

For eating out, Beaune has a number of fine restaurants, including the more expensive L'Ecusson which for some reason has lost a Michelin star, although it remains a top place for innovative food. Booking is recommended in Beaune's fine Ma Cuisine. On the D18 approach to Pernand-Vergelesses, look out for Le Charlemagne.

The Côte de Beaune

S outh of Beaune you find the most famous white wine villages in Burgundy. The Côte d'Or tends to edge into the side valleys, and in this rolling tide of vines you can roam the plain and then go up the slopes to discover villages hidden by the ridges and folds of the landscape. You won't just find Chardonnay. Outside Puligny, there's hardly a village here that doesn't make some red wine, often relatively inexpensive, and the Pinot Noir vines are often old.

Travelling around (see map p.84)
This route begins in the little-visited plain and loops up into the Hautes-Côtes de Beaune. Beginning the "wrong" side of the A6 motorway there's an 11km (7-mile) detour from Beaune to Ste-Marie-la-Blanche on the D970, via Bligny-lès Beaune and Tailly, down the N74 to Chassagne-Montrachet, then a switchback back to Beaune via Puligny, Meursault, Volnay, and Pommard, with optional meanders up the slopes – up the Gamay Valley to St-Aubin, to St-Romain via Auxey-Duresses, and finally a longer detour up to Meloisey and Nantoux.

Ste Marie la Blanche and Bligny-lès Beaune
You may wonder that winemaking down in the plain of the Saône can be done well, and be surprised that it is done at all, but just 90ha – which include the commune of Levernois – remain of vineyards that once extended over 600 ha, originally planted with now-banned hybrid varieties.

During the 1980s, a Ste Marie la Blanche grower replanted with Pinor Noir and Chardonnay, both of which cost little more than €5. The estate belongs to Roger and Joel Remy (4 rue du Paradis, tel: 03 80 26 60 80).

Bligny-lès-Beaune
In Bligny-lès-Beaune, 9 km (5.6 miles) away, Cathérine and Claude Marechal (6 route de Chalon, 21200 Bligny-lès-Beaune, tel: 03 80 21 44 37), have a medium-sized estate that takes in most of the appellations fringing Beaune (see previous chapter) and, from their home village of Bligny, their good-value Cuvée Gravel. Also try Domaine Jean Guiton (4 route de Pommard, 21200 Bligny-lès-Beaune, tel: 03 80 26 82 88).

LEFT *Model patients: dummies in Beaune's Hôtel-Dieu – the phrase simply means "General Hospital" in French.*

BELOW *Domaine des Comtes Lafon: superb Meursault, grown Biodynamically.*

Tailly

Tailly doesn't make wine, but how about its Archeodrome, which was opened in 1972 at the same time as the Autoroute du Soleil? The Archeodrome is a permanent exhibition of human habitation, from the Neolithic to the Gallo-Roman period, and it was inspired by discoveries made while building an autoroute near Dijon.

The emphasis is on reconstructions, including a striking facsimile of Caesar's siege fortifications outside Alésia (Aire de Beaune-Tailly, 21190 Meursault, tel: 03 80 26 87 00, www.archeodrome-bourgogne.com).

Chassagne and Puligny

Why not take a ten-minute spin down the N74, letting the famous names flash past, and then work back up again, starting with Chassagne, halfway up the hill that's called, rather hyperbolically, La Grande Montagne?

Chassagne and its neighbour Puligny share the world's most famous white vineyard. The 8ha of Le Montrachet are divided almost equally between the two communes – Puligny has two ares more, (one are = 0.01ha). The addition of "Montrachet" came into force at the same

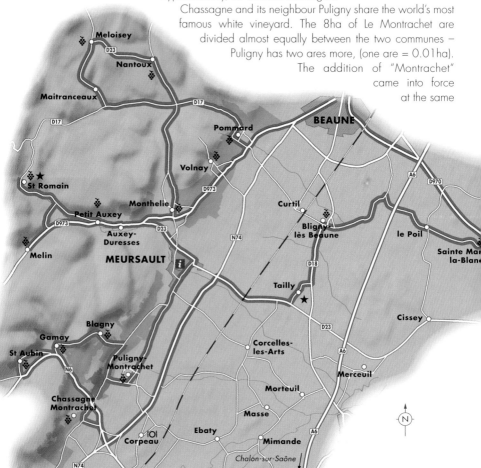

0 1 Km	
0 1 mile	

      Grand cru vineyard

      Premier cru vineyard

      Côte de Beaune

Allow a few days to seriously indulge yourself in this wonderland of white wine

time: November 27, 1879. Puligny is grander-looking, but if you want to buy from independent growers, focus on Chassagne.

Chassagne, once mainly a red wine village, was overlooked by outsiders who only began buying it when the white wine boom of the 1970s and 1980s took off. As a result it remains a village of small-scale *vignerons* who own the usual scattered patchwork of holdings, and sell directly to their customers rather than to a négociant.

The extended family

Chassagne is held together by typically Burgundian networks. One of these is intermarriage. Many of the best producers are called either Gagnard or Morey, or some hyphenated version of either. It would be interesting to buy a couple of bottles from each of the members of one or other family and note the similarities and differences. "We all take roughly the same approach," Bernard Morey told me. "But it's like cooking – no too families make the same dish in exactly the same way."

Head for the village wines

A village called Montrachet is not going to offer many bargains, and there are not one but two châteaux, but this still feels quite a democratic place. Collectors all but come to blows to acquire the *grand cru* wines of the legendary Domaine Ramonet (15 rue de Puits, tel: 03 80 21 30 88), but you can visit, by appointment of course, and buy red and white village wines and Aligoté.

Two big names in Puligny

There are two grand domaines in Puligny-Montrachet: Leflaive (place des Marronniers, 21190 Puligny-Montrachet, tel: 03 80 21 30 13) and Etienne Sauzet (11 rue de Poiseul, 2190 Puligny-Montrachet, tel: 03 80 21 32 10), both of whose wines are heavily oversubscribed. Neither offers direct sales or visits. Chartron et Trébuchet is the other local négociant based in Puligny-Montrachet.

The Leflaive cousins

Olivier Leflaive now concentrates on the négociant business – called, oddly enough, Olivier Leflaive – that he started in 1985, leaving his cousin Anne-Claude in charge of Domaine Leflaive. Don't confuse the two: you can buy from Olivier Leflaive, but not from the domaine. With some input from Jean-Claude Rateau (*see* p.77) Anne-Claude has made all 22ha Biodynamic. In 2003, unable to expand in the Côte d'Or, she bought 9ha in the Mâconnais at Verzé (*see* p.116). She has also been a moving force in the Terre et Vins organization which is currently campaigning against any moves to allow genetically modified vines in *appellation contrôlée* wines.

GROWERS IN CHASSAGNE

THREE GAGNARDS:
Domaine Blain-Gagnard
route de Santenay
21190 Chassagne-Montrachet
Tel: 03 80 21 34 07 (A1)

Domaine R. Fontaine-Gagnard
19 route de Santenay
21190 Chassagne-Montrachet
Tel: 03 80 21 35 50 (A1)

Domaine J-N. Gagnard
9 place des Noyers
21190 Chassagne-Montrachet
Tel: 03 80 21 31 86 (A1)

THREE MOREYS:
Domaine Bernard Morey
3 rue de Morgeot
21190 Chassagne-Montrachet
Tel: 03 80 21 32 13 (A1)

Domaine Jean-Marc Morey
3 rue Principale
21190 Chassagne-Montrachet
Tel: 03 80 21 32 62 (A1)

Domaine Marc Morey et Fils
3 rue Charles Pacquelin
21190 Chassagne-Montrachet
Tel: 03 80 21 30 11 (A1)

OTHER STARS:
Domaine Guy Amiot et Fils
13 rue du Grand Puits
21190 Chassagne-Montrachet
Tel: 03 80 21 38 62 (A1)

Domaine Vincent Dancer
23 route de Santenay
21190 Chassagne-Montrachet
Tel: 03 80 21 94 48 (A1)

Michel Colin-Deleger
3 impasse des Crets
21190 Chassagne-Montrachet
Tel: 03 80 21 32 72 (A1)

Domaine Bernard Moreau
3 route de Chagny
21190 Chassagne-Montrachet
Tel: 03 80 21 33 70 (A1)

PRICES: white is expensive, red often moderate

ABOVE *Domaine Leflaive, run by Anne-Claude Leflaive.*

RIGHT *The art of the roundabout, in Puligny.*

The Sauzet siblings

The Sauzet estate was split in 1990 between Jean-Marc Boillot, a grandson of Etienne (1903–75) (*see above*) and Jean-Marc's sister Jeannine, married to Gérard Boudot. Boudot now buys in grapes to make up for the lost vineyards. Today Sauzet labels include the word Domaine only if the wines are from the directly owned vineyards – just 8ha.

Taste, but buy elsewhere

The municipal *caveau* (9 rue Charles Paquelin, tel: 03 80 21 38 13) is worth visiting. Bearing in mind that few wines here are cheap you're recommended to taste at the *caveau*, and buy a few bottles, before committing yourself to buying case-loads at individual growers.

St-Aubin and Gamay

The old Paris-Lyon road crests the Côte here and south-bound travellers get a first panorama of the vineyards. St-Aubin clusters round a Romanesque church and an old Roman road that continues on to Gamay. St-Aubin's whites are very good but these days there's little below €12. The top names are Hubert Lamy (tel: 03 80 21 32 55), Patrick Miolane on the main road (tel : 03 80 21 31 94), Gérard Thomas (rue Perrières, tel: 03 80 21 32 57), and the Prudhon family, which regularly provides the village with its mayors (place de l'Eglise, tel: 03 80 21 31 33).

Gamay's Romanesque castle (restored in the nineteenth century) is linked with the crusading Seigneur du May, who supposedly brought the Gamay grape back with him. There's little if any Gamay planted here today, but there's at least one outstanding grower in Jean-Claude Bachelet (1 rue de la

Fontaine, tel: 03 80 21 31 01, http://jcbachelet.free.fr). This estate, which dates back three centuries, these days grows mainly red and white St-Aubin and Chassagne *premiers crus*. Also try Gilles Bouton (24 rue de la Fontenotte, 21190 St-Aubin, 03 80 21 32 63).

Meursault

Meursault has no *grand cru* vineyards, but this large village claims to be the *Capitale des Grands Vins Blancs de Bourgogne*. It is home to the Paulée de Meursault, which concludes the three days of feasting that make up November's Trois Glorieuses weekend (*see* p.14). This is a handsome place, built from gleaming white limestone, and its 50m (164-foot) high fifteenth-century church spire dominates the vineyards from afar.

(Fairly) amazing but true

Meursault's name refers to its little stream, the Ruisseau des Cloux, so narrow as to be just a mouse's leap – in Latin *muris saltus* – from bank to bank. The town hall is the old castle, rebuilt twice between the fourteenth and nineteenth centuries. The church of St Nicolas was originally its chapel.

The wines

For many, Meursault *is* white burgundy. The American barrel importer Mel Knox points out that the cooper who supplied Puligny toasted the cask staves to get them to bend, whereas his counterpart in Meursault used steam, which explains some of the differences in taste and style: the terroir explains the rest, as is always the case (or should be) in Burgundy. Meursault should be rich and hedonistic; tasters talk about butteriness and hazelnuts, or even cinnamon. There's also often a certain smokiness, or a vegetal note, which may sound a bit dodgy but is delicious. This is comfort wine with Burgundian minerality.

GROWERS IN MEURSAULT

Alain Coche-Bizouard
5 rue de Mazeray
21190 Meursault
Tel: 03 80 21 28 41
(*B/C2*)
Mainly inexpensive appellations.

Domaine des Comtes Lafon
5 rue Pierre Joigneaux
21190 Meursault
Tel: 03 80 21 22 17
(*B/C2*)
The top estate.

Arnaud Ente
12 rue Mazeray
21190 Meursault (*B/C2*)

Domaine J-P. Fichet
2 rue Sudot
21190 Meursault
Tel: 03 80 21 28 51
(*B/C2*)
Young and going places.

Patrick Javillier
impasse des Acacias
21190 Meursault
Tel: 03 80 21 27 87
(*B/C2*)
Try Cuvée Oligocene.

Domaine Joseph Matrot
12 rue de Martray
21190 Meursault
Tel: 03 80 21 20 13 (*B/C2*)
A local legend.

Morey-Blanc
13 rue Mouchoux
21190 Meursault
Tel: 03 80 21 21 03 (*B/C2*)
Morey also makes the wine at Domaine Leflaive.

Domaine Pascal Prunier-Bonheur
23 rue des Plantes
21190 Meursault
Tel: 03 80 21 66 56
(*B/C2*)
Pascal has recently moved to Meursault.

PRICES: expensive

**GROWERS IN AUXEY-DURESSES
AND MONTHELIE**

Jean-Pierre Diconne
rue de la Velle
21190 Auxey Duresses
Tel: 03 80 21 25 60 *(C2)*
Good-value Auxey.

Domaine Paul Garaudet
rue Cimetière
21190 Monthelie
Tel: 03 80 21 28 78 *(C2)*
Classy wines here.

Domaine A. et B. Labry
21190 Auxey Duresses
Tel: 03 80 21 21 60 *(C2)*
Good *crémant*.

Jean et Gilles Lafouge
rue Dessous
21190 Auxey Duresses
Tel: 03 80 21 20 92 *(C2)*
Can be superb value.

Henri Latour
21190 Auxey Duresses
Tel: 03 80 21 65 49 *(C2)*
Successful wines.

Domaine Monthelie-Douhairet
Grande Rue
21190 Monthelie
Tel: 03 80 21 63 13 *(C2)*
Plenty of character.

Annick Parent
rue Château Gaillard
21190 Monthelie
Tel: 03 80 21 21 98 *(C2)*
Good, if a bit tough.

Michel Prunier
21190 Auxey-Duresses
Tel: 03 80 21 21 05 *(C2)*
First among equals.

OTHER PRUNIERS:
Vincent, Tel: 03 80 21 27
77; **J-P. et L.,** Tel: 03 80 21
23 91

Domaine Eric de Suremain
Château de Monthelie
21190 Monthelie
Tel: 03 80 21 23 32 *(C2)*

PRICES: moderate

How to win on price and quality

Meursault prices are currently around €20 per bottle. For cheaper white burgundies I'd look to St-Aubin, St-Romain or Auxey-Duresses if you want elegance, or try a simple Bourgogne Blanc from a top Meursault or Chassagne grower. These will be made with the same care as the greater wines, and can sometimes come from some pretty good vineyards, too: leading growers often like to put young-vine wine from village vineyards into their Bourgogne Blanc, keeping only that from really mature vines for their top labels.

Auxey-Duresses

This handsome village at the bottom of the valley that winds its way up to La Rochepot (see p.97) is a place to look for bargains, since a hard-to-pronounce name can take several euros off the price of a wine – the correct way to pronounce Auxey is "Aussey". Its reds can need a little time to soften; the whites are good Meursault alternatives. They are often made by growers called Prunier.

One local winemaker not feeling the pinch is Lalou Bize-Leroy, the owner of Domaine and Maison Leroy, whose offices are here. Many think Leroy – another all-Biodynamic estate – is the greatest name in Burgundy.

There are two grand houses in the village – the Château de Digoine and the Château de Melin – and there's a fine sixteenth-century triptych with scenes of the life of the Virgin Mary in the gothic church of St Martin.

St-Romain

St-Romain's growers can thank Roland Thévenin (1905–90) for belonging to the Côte de Beaune and not to the Hautes-Côtes. This négociant lobbied successfully for a separate appellation and got it in 1947. He cleverly tagged St-Romain "*mon village*", and made it in effect his brand.

St-Romain is again internationally known thanks to the success of the barrel-maker François Frères (tel: 03 80 21 23 33, www.francois freres.com). The weather up here is ideal for the long slow process of weathering oak staves outdoors. Finally, St-Romain is the base of Lalou Bize-Leroy's personal estate, Domaine d'Auvenay, with its scattered portfolio of vineyard holdings.

St-Romain's wines are more expensive than any old Hautes-Côtes de Beaune, but are they better? Yes – particularly the whites, perhaps because of the motivation given to growers by being part of the Côte de Beaune. The best producers in the village include Christophe Buisson (tel: 03 80 21 63 92), Domaine de Chassorney (tel: 03 80 21 65 55), Alain Gras (tel: 03 80 21 27 83), and the Biodynamic pioneer Thierry

Guyot (tel: 03 80 21 27 52). St-Romain has drawn people to settle here for at least five thousand years, and the town hall (Grande Rue, tel: 03 80 21 20 16), has a exhibition about the village's prehistory, which is open during the summer. The Upper Village is built on a spur of rock in a natural amphitheatre of cliffs; the layout of its fifteenth-century church echoes this pattern. A well-marked footpath leads to the remains of the village's medieval castle.

Leave your car in Monthelie

Another picturesque little village, and another little valley, La Combe Danay. Rather than driving to Volnay and Pommard, you could walk, starting from the bottom of the valley and climbing the slopes to the north, then taking the bridleway, the Grande Randonée 76, or carrying on up until you can see the Côte – north of Beaune, then coming back down through the vineyards. Pommard is only a little over 1km (0.6 miles) further on, and from there the return walk to Monthelie is little more than 3km (1.9 miles). So, it is advisable to allow a couple of hours for the round trip.

Monthelie, pronounced "Mont'lie", is a name that I find creates pleasurable anticipation on a label, though often followed by some slight disappointment at the price. The version from the Coche-Bizouards, who are bsed in Meursault, ages particularly well, I find.

Or keep your car and drive to Nantoux

A 5km (3-mile) drive takes you to Nantoux, one of the prettiest villages in the Hautes-Côtes de Beaune, with a medieval church, no fewer than thirteen perpetually gushing springs, and a large number of growers called Montchovet. Didier and Christine Montchovet are Biodynamic (tel: 03 80 26 03 13).

Also recommended: Philippe Germain (tel: 03 80 26 05 63, www.philippegermain.com) who also offers a *gîte*. In the village of Meloisey, a couple of kilometres (1.2 miles) away, is one of the most thriving Hautes-Côtes producers, Denis Carré (tel: 03 80 26 02 21).

Volnay

Of the great wine villages of the Côte de Beaune, Volnay is at the highest altitude. There's a doggerel rhyme, quoted in a local walking guide (*Balades en Bourgogne*, Editions Pelican) which goes: "*En dépit de Pommard et Meursault, C'est toujours Volnay le plus haut*" ("Despite Pommard and Meursault, Volnay is always the highest").

Its soft red wines, conventionally classed as "feminine", contrast with the tougher, wines from its neighbour Pommard. There's a traditional rivalry between the two villages.

GROWERS IN POMMARD AND VOLNAY

POMMARD: Domaine François Parent/A-F. Gros
route Ivry
Tel: 03 80 22 05 50 **(C/D3)**
See main text.

Domaine du Comte Armand
7 rue de la Mairie
Tel: 03 80 24 70 50
A serious player with superb wine – now Biodynamic

Domaine de Courcel,
rue Notre Dame
Tel: 03 80 22 10 64
Four-centuries-old

Jean-Marc Boillot
route d'Autun
Tel: 03 80 24 97 57
Boillot inherited part of the holdings of Sauzet in Puligny.

VOLNAY: Domaine Michel Lafarge
rue de la Combe
Tel: 03 80 21 61 61 **(C2)**
Top-ranking.

Domaine de Montille
rue Pied de la Vallée
Tel: 03 80 21 62 67 **(C2)**
Organic methods.

Domaine de la Pousse d'Or
rue de la Chapelle
Tel: 03 80 21 61 33 **(C2)**
Formerly the Potel estate. New management, and a natural approach.

Rossignol – there are nineteen are in the telephone book. **Rossignol-Février** and **Rossignol-Jeanniard,** both rue de Mont, Tel: 03 80 21 64 23 and 03 80 21 64 23 respectively.

PRICES: a few moderately priced bargains; most *premiers crus* are expensive

This is the home of the d'Angervilles. Burgundy may seem overstuffed with "great names" and "legends". But, Jacques Marquis d'Angerville, who died in 1952, put his livelihood on the line in the 1920s by campaigning against mis-labelling by the négociants. He was one of Baudouin's first allies (*see* p.7), and later became journalist and wine importer, Frank Schoonmaker's chief talent-spotter in Burgundy. His son, also Jacques Marquis d'Angerville, died in 2003; he too campaigned for the growers, and created a strain of Pinot Noir called "Pinot Fin", notable for its low yields and high quality. The estate is near the fourteenth-century village church; it isn't geared up for direct sales to customers (tel: 03 80 21 61 75).

Pommard

Is there a village in Burgundy whose wine wasn't the favourite of some famous historical figure? Pommard claims Victor Hugo, Louis XV and Henri IV (though Givry in the Côte Chalonnaise is plastered with signs staking its claim to Henri IV…).

Today, Pommard, despite its mellifluous name, is rather a hard sell – the wines, some from iron-rich soils, need ageing to soften; what's more there isn't, as in Volnay, a critical mass of famous producers. But this is one of the great red wine villages of the Côte de Beaune, so the wines aren't cheap.

But some are affordable – for example from François Parent and his wife Anne-François Gros. Their marriage gave them access to an unusual spread of vineyards, from Vosne-Romanée and Chambolle-Musigny to Corton, Ladoix, Pommard, St Romain (white) – and a Bourgogne Rouge that the couple swear should be a Pommard.

The southern fringes of the Côte d'Or: Santenay, Maranges, and Couchois

. . . .

H ere we definitely leave the beaten track and head off into little-known corners. Santenay until recently was more famous as a spa than for its wines; Maranges and Couches have became *appellations contrôlées* in their own right, but they could still fairly be called obscure. To understand this region means digging below surface impressions.

Water and iron

Santenay and Couches were shaped by more than the quality of their vineyards' soil. "Santenay-les-Bains" was developed in the late nineteenth century. The waters rise from deep geological faults, and have the highest levels of lithium (an anti-manic-depressive medication) of anywhere in Europe.

The region around Couches was transformed earlier when Schneider, a Le Creusot steelmaker, developed the local iron deposits. Couche's vineyards had new outlets: the iron-miners, the steel town of Le Creusot and the coalminers of Montceau-les-Mines. The foundations for the economic boom had already been laid. France's Canal du Centre, built in the eighteenth century to join the Atlantic with the Mediterranean, today allows pleasure boats to travel between Monchanin, near a TGV rail station, and Chalon-sur-Saône – Burgundy's second biggest town – via Maranges, Santenay, and Chagny.

Travelling around (*see* map p.93)

The canal follows a tributary of the Saône, the Dheune, as far as Chagny – the starting point for a route which takes us to Santenay, Cheilly-lès-Maranges, St-Sernin-du-Plain, Couches, Dracy-lès-Couches, Dezize-les-Maranges, Change, and Marchezeuil, finishing at La Rochepot. But beforehand, follow the Dheune from Chagny on a 10km (6-mile) round trip to Demigny (not to be confused with nearby Remigny, *C1*).

Demigny is a small, attractive village with its own little-known vineyards. But the point is to visit a talented négociant called François d'Allaines (La Corvée du Paquier, 71150 Demigny, tel: 03 85 49 90 16, www.dallaines.com). It began as a specialist in the Côte Chalonnaise, and this is a good place to begin getting your head around southern Burgundy.

BELOW *A stake in the land: until recently vine-growing was often overshadowed by heavy industry in this part of Burgundy.*

Santenay

Pronounced "Sant'nay" (of course). These vineyards face due south, at the point where the long east-facing slope finally wheels round to face the valley of the Dheune. The better drained vineyards on the higher ground produce more delicate wines – and good whites. Santenay's red wines are mainly firm, with flavours of red fruits, almonds, and violets; some are quite like Côte de Nuits reds.

Two stars, newish and very new

Vincent Girardin, one of three Girardins here, made his first vintage, in 1982, of 650 cases of wine. In 2002, he made 50,000, and took an eighteen-year-lease which gave him access to such *grands crus* as Chevalier Montrachet, Bâtard-Montrachet, and Bienvenues-Bâtard-Montrachet. Girardin has been a huge success with American customers and critics who admire his clean, modern style. In 2002, he moved to a new winery in Meursault (chemin des Champs Lins, 21190 Meursault, tel: 03 80 20 81 00).

Jean-Marc Vincent made his first vintage as recently as 1998, but has caught the critics' attention with a mixture of scrupulous vineyard work – using organic and Biodynamic approaches – and by fermenting whole bunches of red grapes together with their stems. It's very Burgundian to use a technique associated with great, long-lived wines in such relatively low-status appellations as Santenay and Auxey-Duresses. (3 rue Ste Agathe, 21590 Santenay, tel: 03 80 20 67 37.) There's unlikely to be anything to sell, but try the Cave des Vieilles Vignes (22 place du Jet d'Eau, 21590 Santenay, tel: 03 80 20 69 33).

Visiting Santenay

There is Bas-Santenay, which is the main village, Haut-Santenay, and the hamlet of St Jean, with its small gothic church. The Château de Philippe-le-Hardi takes its name from the first of the Valois dukes (1363–1404), though parts of the building are centuries earlier. It's also a huge wine estate (94ha) owned by a bank. Two pedantic notes: the Burgundian polychromatic roof tiles are modern; and I can't believe that the two 400-year-old plane trees can be that old – they'd have had to have been among the first specimens of *Platanus orientalis* to be introduced to France.

Other amusements

The Casino des Sources has seven table games including blackjack, and French and English roulette, as well as 150 slot machines. There is a "correct" dress code. (9 avenue des Sources, 21590 Santenay, tel: 03 80 26 22 44.)

The Voie Verte is the northern end of 80km (50 miles) of disused railway, converted to a cycle track. From here you can cycle the 22km (14 miles) to Chalon-sur-Saône along the Canal du Centre.

Cheilly-lès-Maranges

Here, according to Alexandre Dumas, we are in Burgundy's mini-Switzerland, overlooked by the "three peaks", the Mont de Rème, the Montagne des Trois Croix, and Mont de Rome-Château. Dezize, Cheilly, and Sampigny were granted double-barrelled status between 1897 and 1899 ("lès" means "near to"). The point was to link the villages with their best-known vineyards – even if the vineyards called En Marange, Les Maranges, and Les Plantes-en-Marange don't quite have the recognition factor of Montrachet and Chambertin.

Since 1988, there's been a single Maranges appellation for wines from Cheilly along with those of Dezize and Sampigny (see p.96 for some Dezize growers). No one's exactly sure

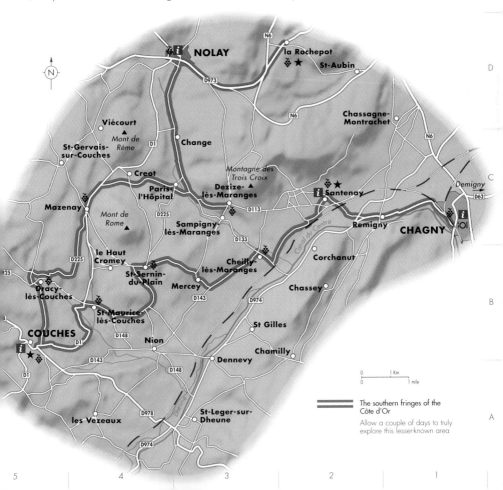

The southern fringes of the Côte d'Or

Allow a couple of days to truly explore this lesser-known area

RIGHT *Young vine leaves escaping from protective netting.*

FAR RIGHT *The other end of the cycle: harvesting boxes awaiting the new crop.*

LOCAL INFORMATION

Office de Tourisme
Gare SNCF
21590 Santenay
Tel: 03 80 20 63 15

Office de Tourisme
24 ave de la République
21340 Nolay
Tel: 03 80 21 80 73

Office de Tourisme
2 rue des Halles,
71150 Chagny
Tel: 03 85 87 25 95

Syndicat d'Initiative
3 Grande Rue
71490 Couches
Tel: 03 85 49 69 47

what the name "Maranges" refers to, although it may be a dialect word for the wild carrots that grow locally.

In terms of terrain, Maranges covers 170ha of vineyards that face due south under the slopes of the Montagne des Trois Croix (C3). The wines are unusual in Burgundy in that they come from gravel soils, like the Saône Valley wines described on p.83. Until recently the négoce bought virtually the whole crop, for blending with light reds such as St-Romain or Chorey-lès-Beaune, and sold the result as Côtes de Beaune-Villages.

On their own Maranges reds need some time to soften, but they are brilliant value – around €7 for village wines, and usually less than €10 for *premiers crus*. Pablo Chevrot, who's just taken over from his father at one of the best Maranges estates, suggests a five-year wait, and then trying these reds with fish.

Pablo has already made one or two changes at Domaine Chevrot, including ending his father Fernand's use of cultivated yeasts. Fernand and Cathérine continue to manage the *gîte* here which would be a good base from which to explore the area (19 route de Couches, 71150 Cheilly-lès-Maranges, tel: 03 85 91 10, www.chevrot.fr).

Cheilly's grand house is the Château de Mercey, which the local Berger-Rive family sold to the négociant Antonin Rodet in 1998. Rodet has opted to focus on the appellation Hautes-Côtes de Beaune so that it can legally use the lyre training system. The château is open for visits and sales (71150 Cheilly-lès-Maranges, tel: 03 85 91 13 19).

St-Sernin-du-Plain

A short drive and we're no longer in the Côte d'Or but are entering the Couchois – an appellation created as recently as 2001, rather against the wishes of local growers, who wanted to sell their wine under the better-known name of Hautes-Côtes de Beaune. They've had to agree to reduce their yields and try to go upmarket, and they don't have it easy.

The Liassic (Early Jurassic) soils produce light red wines but with marked tannins that need years to soften, and customers who expect to be able to pull the cork right away on a €6 or €7 bottle don't always get the point.

The leading grower here in this ancient town – built on the site of a Roman settlement – is Domaine des Trois Monts, Daniel Pichard (8 rue des Grandes Plants, 71570 St-Sernin-du-Plain, tel: 03 85 45 58 10).

St-Maurice-lès-Couches

This small commune has at least two significant producers. Marie-Anne et Jean-Claude Dessendre own the twelfth-century Tour Bajole in Couches, currently home to a restaurant (see p.97). Their domaine, Domaine de la Tour Bajole is named after the tower (Ombrots, 71490 St-Maurice-lès-Couches, tel: 03 85 45 52 90). It's also worth visiting the Domaine du Puits Fleuri (4 rue Marchez, 71490 St-Maurice-lès-Couches, tel: 03 85 49 68 44).

Couches

The valley below Couches is dominated by its eleventh-century castle with thirteenth-century battlements, which is locally associated with Marguerite de Bourgogne, the repudiated wife of Louis X. Although Marguerite's death was publicly announced in 1315, according to local legend she was taken in by her family at Couches and lived on, in seclusion, for a further eighteen years. The castle is open to visitors in the summer months (tel: 03 85 45 57 99, or check website www.perso. wanadoo.fr/richez/Bourgogne /Couches.htm for visiting hours).

You could leave your car in the town and walk across to Dracy, taking the footpath that crosses the ridge separating Couches' little river, the Vielle, from Dracy's river, the Ruyisseau de Corcelle. There are two important growers here: the château (see above), and Jean Musso, who's an organic pioneer. Musso's cellar (tel: 03 85 96 18 61) is not here in

**Domaine Bernard Bachelet
et Fils**
rue Maranges
71150 Dezize-lès-
Maranges
Tel: 03 85 91 16 11 *(C3)*
A big estate – the largest
in Maranges, with holdings
in Chassagne, Santenay,
Meursault, and as far north
as Gevrey-Chambertin.
Some great stuff.

**Domaine Maurice
Charleux**
1 Petite Rue, 71150
Dezize-lès-Maranges
Tel: 03 85 91 15 15 *(C3)*
Fabulous value from very
old vines.

**Domaine Edmonde
Monnot et Fils**
rue de Borgy, 71150
Dezize-les-Maranges
Tel: 03 85 91 16 12 *(C3)*
Monnot's Hautes-Côtes
de Beaune holdings are in
labour-intensive, low-
trained *vignes bas*.

**Domaine Claude Nouveau
Marchezeuil**
21340 Change
Tel: 03 85 91 13 34 *(C3)*
Hedonistic wines, and not
much over €10.

**Domaine de la Confrerie
Jean Pauchard et Fils**
37 rue Perraudin
21340 Nolay
Tel: 03 80 21 89 23 *(C3)*
Try the Hautes-Côtes.

PRICES: inexpensive

Couches, but 32km (20 miles) away at Sassangy, just west of
Montagny and Buxy on the D977.

Mazenay

Mazenay, 3km (2 miles) to the northwest, used to be a village
of 1,000 inhabitants, and home to several iron-ore mines,
served by a railway branch line. Between Mazenay and St-
Sernin runs a path climbing the Mont de Rome-Château, which
is named, apparently, after Romulus, the legendary founder of
Rome. Romulus' twin Remus gives his name to the Mont de
Rème, due north beyond the village of Creot. On the uplands,
the poor soils are rich in wildflowers and wildlife.

As for wines in Mazenay, the négociant Marinot-Verdun's
Caves de Mazenay (not in this case the name of a cooperative)
offers tastings of a wide spread of appellations under the
compelling slogan "Grands Vins à Petits Prix" (71510 St-Sernin-
du-Plain, tel: 03 85 49 67 19).

Paris l'Hôpital

Back into the Hautes-Côtes de Beaune, and after Mont Rome,
another place that sounds like a capital city. A medieval knight
whose wife, after insisting he did not go crusading, founded a
charitable institution on a piece of ground called Paris. Few
local growers sell directly but try Domaine les Vignes Blaches
(Le Bourg, 71150 Paris l'Hopital, tel: 03 80 91 14 56).

Dezize-lès-Maranges

Dezize lies beneath the Mont de Sène, also known as the
Montagne des Trois Croix, and a short climb to its summit
rewards you with a view over the valley of the Cosanne. This

RIGHT *Here as elsewhere,
old vines = low yields =
good wine.*

peak was a pre-Roman burial place, then became the site of a temple of Mercury; it now gets its name from three nineteenth-century crosses.

Change and Nolay

Change is another attractive village, with a water-mill on the Cosanne. The best grower is halfway up the Mont de Rème (p.93, C4). Before visiting him at Marcheseuil, halfway up the slope, check the view from the summit.

Nolay is the capital of the Hautes-Côtes de Beaune; its medieval buildings include a fourteenth-century corn-market and many half-timbered houses.

From Nolay walk or drive north via Vauchignon by the D111 to the 50m (164-foot) waterfall at the beauty spot called the Cirque du Bout du Monde. Less dramatically there's a reservoir near the town with supervised bathing.

La Rochepot

From its appearance the Château de la Rochepot could be a Bavarian-style nineteenth-century fantasy, but it is in fact a pretty faithful nineteenth-century reconstruction of a medieval original destroyed during the Revolution. Just outside is Denis Fouquerand, one of the Hautes-Côtes pioneers of *crémant* (Domaine Fouquerand Père et Fils, 21340 La Rochepot, tel: 03 80 21 71). On the main road from Nolay is another gifted grower, Michel Serveau (21340 La Rochepot, tel: 03 80 21 70 24).

Relax and indulge

There are good restaurants in Nolay, Couches, and Santenay, which combine good fish (that, unfortunately, has to come all the way from the English Channel) and locally reared pork, goose, lamb, etc. *See* right for contact details of Le Burgonde, La Tour Bajolle, and Le Terroir, respectively.

Meanwhile, in the rather low-profile area of Chagny you can find Burgundy's greatest restaurant, which is also an hotel – Lameloise (*see* right for details). To eat here costs around €100 per person; and to stay, around twice that. However, even millionaires may sometimes feel like a break from three-star eating – if so, then try Le Grenier à Sel, a reliable wood-grill place housed, as the name suggests, in a former salt store.

WHERE TO STAY AND EAT

Lameloise
36 place d'Armes
71150 Chagny
Tel: 03 85 87 65 65

Hôtel de la Ferté
11 boulevard de la Liberté
71150 Chagny
www.hotelferte.com

Hôtel de la Poste
17 rue de la Poste
71150 Chagny
Tel: 03 85 87 64 40

Auberge de la Musardière
30 route de Chalon
71150 Chagny
Tel: 03 85 87 04 97

Les Trois Maures
4 place de la République
71490 Couches
Tel: 03 85 49 63 93
www.hoteldestroismaures.com

Hôtel de la Halle
21340 Nolay
Tel: 03 80 21 76 37

Le Grenier à Sel
3 rue Marc Boillet
71150 Chagny
Tel: 03 85 87 09 10

Le Terroir
19 place du Jet d'Eau
21590 Santenay
Tel: 03 80 20 63 47

Restaurant de la Tour Bajolle
71490 Couches
Tel: 03 85 45 54 54

Le Burgonde
35 rue de la République
21340 Nolay
Tel: 03 80 21 71 25

The Côte Chalonnaise

O n paper there's no contest: the Côte d'Or has the famous wines that people have heard of... it's twice the length, it's packed with sights to see, but I'm not sure I wouldn't prefer to spend time with the poor relative. This region exemplifies the Burgundian qualities of straightforwardness and lack of pretention. When people make a fuss over a Montagny or a Rully you can be sure that it's simply because they're knocked out by the quality of the wine – not that there's a famous name on the label.

No common style

It's easiest to define the Côte Chalonnaise by saying what it isn't. Chalon-sur-Saône is not a wine town like Nuits-St-Georges or Beaune. Even the very phrase "wine town" feels a little forced: the vineyards between Chagny in the north and Buxy in the south aren't a "côte" in the sense of the unbroken sea of vines familiar further north. Until recently, in fact, this was called the Region de Mercurey. It's hard to pinpoint a common style, which is perhaps one reason that the Côte Chalonnaise appellation has never taken off: each of the villages has a strong, and quite distinct personality.

Rise and fall

In some ways the Côte Chalonnaise is what the Côte d'Or was like before the wines became so expensive. The vineyards don't form a monoculture, but take their place with other crops and with the famous off-white Charolais cattle. But wine has helped preserve the life of the countryside here; the relatively high price of grapes has helped farmers to make a living and escape the flight to the towns – the process the French call *la desertification*. The international success of Chardonnay in the 1980s encouraged growers to plant more and more – but in the last few years the bubble has burst, leading to many cellars of unsold stocks, to bankruptcies, and to demonstrations on the streets of Chalon.

One thing I like about this region's wine culture is that it exemplifies the typically Burgundian qualities of

BELOW *Buzzing with activity: honey and wine can go together in these parts.*

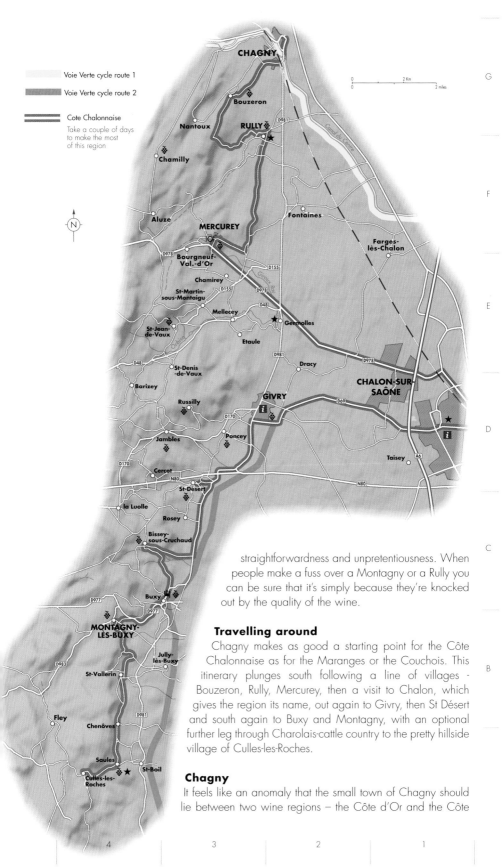

CHAGNY

Bouzeron

Nantoux

RULLY

Chamilly

Aluze

MERCUREY

Fontaines

Farges-
lès-Chalon

Bourgneuf-
Val.-d'Or

Chamirey

St-Martin-
sous-Montaigu

Mellecey

Germolles

St-Jean
de-Vaux

Etaule

St-Denis
-de-Vaux

Barizey

Dracy

CHALON-SUR-
SAÔNE

Russilly

GIVRY

Jambles

Poncey

Cercot

Taisey

St-Désert

la Luolle

Rosey

Bissey-
sous-Cruchaud

straightforwardness and unpretentiousness. When
people make a fuss over a Montagny or a Rully you
can be sure that it's simply because they're knocked
out by the quality of the wine.

Travelling around

Chagny makes as good a starting point for the Côte
Chalonnaise as for the Maranges or the Couchois. This
itinerary plunges south following a line of villages -
Bouzeron, Rully, Mercurey, then a visit to Chalon, which
gives the region its name, out again to Givry, then St Désert
and south again to Buxy and Montagny, with an optional
further leg through Charolais-cattle country to the pretty hillside
village of Culles-les-Roches.

Buxy

MONTAGNY-
LES-BUXY

Jully-
lès-Buxy

St-Vallerin

Fley

Chenôves

Saules

St-Boil

Culles-les-
Roches

Chagny

It feels like an anomaly that the small town of Chagny should
lie between two wine regions – the Côte d'Or and the Côte

GROWERS IN CHAGNY AND BOUZERON

Domaine Chanzy
1 rue de la Fontaine
71150 Bouzeron
Tel: 03 85 87 23 69 *(G3)*
www.bourgogne-chanzy.com
See main text.

Domaine de la Folie
71150 Chagny
Tel: 03 85 87 18 59
(G2/3)
www.domainedelafolie.com
Rully red and white
premiers crus.

Domaine Pagnotta Père et Fils
1 rue de Chaudenay
71150 Chagny
Tel: 03 85 87 22 08
(G2/3)
Both Bouzeron and Rully.

Domaine A. et P. de Villaine
2 rue de la Fortune
71150 Bouzeron
Tel: 03 85 91 20 50 *(G3)*
www.de-villaine.com
See main text.

PRICES: inexpensive

Chalonnaise – without itself being a wine-producer. Instead, it's a centre of boiler-making and light industry, between the nineteenth-century industrial towns of Le Creusot and Chalon-sur-Saône, with strategic rail and canal links.

But this town is not grimly dedicated to metal-bashing. In Lameloise (*see* p.97), established in the 1920s, it has Burgundy's greatest restaurant; Chagny is also the starting point for a number of walks, along the canal, into the Maranges (*see* p.93), or to Bouzeron and the Montagne de la Folie via a well-marked path. More information on local walks and maps can be obtained from the Chagny Office de Tourisme (2 rue des Halles, tel: 03 85 87 25 95).

On the slopes of the Montagne de la Folie is one of the Côte Chalonnaise's best producers, the Domaine de la Folie (*see* left). Since we're just up the road from Chalon, the birthplace of photography (*see* p.104), it seems appropriate that this estate should have been home to Etienne-Jules Marey (1830–1904), one of the pioneers of the moving film camera.

Bouzeron

In this hillside village – a Roman settlement and later the site of a Cluniac monastery – you may hear that the subsoil is identical to that at Corton (just as in Rully they will tell you that they share the same geology as Puligny-Montrachet. It's the same fragile self-confidence that makes Bruges, Amsterdam and St Petersburg insist that they're the "Venice of the North"). But, when you feel like Aligoté with its mineral and lemon-zest tang – Aligoté is the grape variety stipulated for the Bouzeron appellation, and the best Aligoté comes from here, though it can be grown elsewhere – no Côte d'Or Chardonnay can be any substitute.

The two estates that put Bouzeron on the map, and fought for its appellation, face each other across the main street. They

ABOVE *A passion for window dressing – brightens up the wine villages of the region.*

are Domaine Chanzy (a big concern of 41ha) and the domaine of Aubert and Pamela de Villaine, the part-owners of the Côte d'Or's Domaine de la Romanée-Conti.

Daniel Chanzy is worth a visit, not least because, unusually, he keeps a stock of older red vintages (the Bouzeron is for immediate drinking). His daughter Sophie and son-in-law are scooping up awards as *jeunes talents* (young talents).

The de Villaines' Bouzeron is very good – so too are their red Mercureys and their white Rullys and Côte Chalonnaises. The estate is organic and the grapes hand-picked (as at the DRC); one feature of this property is the use of large oak tuns and concrete vats, as well as the usual Burgundian barrels, to maintain the freshness of these lighter-bodied wines.

If you just want to buy some local wines without a fuss, there's a *caveau* attached to the village café.

Pause for a climb

The Montagne de la Folie lies between Bouzeron and Rully. The bridle-path, the Grande Randonée 76, climbs to its summit. It's well worth the scramble, whichever of the two villages you choose to start from.

Rully

The Côte Chalonnaise begins and ends with white wine villages – although Rully also makes a paleish red. White Rully is not far from white Côte de Beaune in style – utterly likeable. The limestone soils produce something softer and more crowd-pleasing than the flintier Montagny 25km (15 miles) south.

But perhaps Rully's biggest claim to fame is as a sparkling wine centre, where merchants carry out the process of *élaboration* (turning still wine into sparkling) on wines from throughout the Côte Chalonnaise and beyond. Veuve Ambal has been here since 1989; here André Delorme, in 1942, diversified his family wine business into Champagne lookalikes. Veuve Ambal does not receive visitors, but they are welcome at both André Delorme and the smaller but very good Vitteaut-Alberti (*see* right). Try the Delorme rosé.

Ambal was far from the first to put bubbles into burgundy, of course. According to wine writer André Simon, one J. Lausserre of Nuits-St-Georges did it in 1820, making 150,000 bottles that year, his production rising later in the decade to one million bottles.

There was also a mania for bubbles, red, white, and pink, in the early twentieth century. Château Ducru-Beaucaillou, a Bordeaux Second Growth, went sparkling in 1917; the demand was also met by Australia which created its red so-called "sparkling burgundies", now properly rechristened as sparkling Shiraz.

See p.97

GROWERS IN RULLY

Domaine Jean-Claude Brelière
1 place de l'Eglise
71150 Rully
Tel: 03 85 91 22 01
(F/G3)
A hit with, among others, the owners of Lameloise.
See p.97

Domaine Michel Briday
31 Grande Rue
71150 Rully
Tel: 03 85 87 07 90 *(F/G3)*
Rich, complex whites matured on lees.

André Delorme
2 rue de la République
71150 Rully
Tel: 03 85 87 10 12 *(F/G3)*
www.andre-delorme.fr
See main text.

Domaine Vincent Dureuil-Janthial
10 rue Buisserole
71150 Rully
Tel: 03 85 87 26 32 *(F/G3)*
A top contender. Complex, lively wines, very old vines.

Domaine Henri et Paul Jacqueson
5 rue de Chevremont
71150 Rully
Tel: 03 85 87 18 82 *(F/G3)*
Great wines in a full-bloodedly traditionalist way – foot-treading twice a day, and destemming of red grapes only when the stems fail to ripen fully.

Vitteaut-Alberti
20 rue du Pont d'Arrot
71150 Rully
Tel: 03 85 87 23 97
(F/G3)
www.lesvinsfrancais.com/vitteaut-alberti
See main text.

PRICES: inexpensive

ABOVE *Mercurey's main street, which runs west to Couches and Autun.*

RIGHT *French roundabouts are quite funny... until you start telling people how funny they are.*

CYCLE AND SCOOTER HIRE

Cyclo Passion
1 place d l'Eglise
71640 Givry
Tel: 03 85 44 57 55

Hotel le Relais du Montagny
Place du Rond Point
71390 Buxy
Tel: 03 85 94 94 94

Philippe Airault
9 avenue Jean Jaurès
71100 Chalon
Tel: 03 85 48 06 17

Château de Rully

Unusually for Burgundy, the local landmark château, with its chunkily symmetrical medieval keep, is also one of the village's best wine producers. It has been owned by the same family, de Ternay, since the mid-twelfth century, but since 1986 Antonin Rodet has made the wine from the 45ha of vineyards. Don't miss the impressive fifteenth-century kitchens and kitchen equipment (tel: 03 85 87 20 89).

Rully is on the Canal du Centre, meaning that Santenay and Chalon are just a boat ride away.

Mercurey

Mercurey is named after a temple of Mercury – and this, not Nuits-St-Georges or Gevrey-Chambertin, is the single village that produces the most red wine in the whole of Burgundy. Unfortunately, people have been so used to saying what good value it is that it's lost some of its competitive edge.

It's a large village, with a long main road that for once points inland, to Couches and Autun, rather than north-south. At times you feel as if you're in an annex of the Côte d'Or rather than a separate region. This is the headquarters of Antonin Rodet, which has grown from this base to become one of the biggest names in Meursault (where it owns Jacques Prieur), and the Côte de Nuits (where it owns Domaine des Perdrix). The cellar is on the right going towards Couches (*see* right). Another big Côte d'Or name in Mercurey is Faiveley – which owns no less than 70ha, and makes an inexpensive wine I've always thought a benchmark for Burgundian Pinot: La Framboisière. Meanwhile, one of the top makers of Corton is Laurent Juillot, at his cellars on Mercurey's Grande Rue. Nearby is the Caveau St Antoine (121 Grande Rue, 71640 Mercurey, tel: 03 85 98 04 94), a wine shop with a sideline in Belgian beers. The proprietors also offer a small house as a *gîte*, available for rental by the week.

Walking for your wine

One major Mercurey producer, the Château de Chamilly (*see* p.99, F3/4) is 8km (5 miles), in fact could be reached in the course of a walk, leaving town on the D978 and taking the footpath to the village of Aluze, with its high church steeple. On the way you can, if necessary, take shelter in a traditional *cabotte* – the little igloo-like stone houses you find in many of Burgundy's vineyards (and which are featured on the labels of Rémi Rollin in Pernand Vergelesses).

After Aluze, the Domaine du Château de Chamilly (fourteenth century, with seventeenth-century additions) is a further 4km (2.5 miles), reached on the Grande Randonée 7 (Le Château, 71510 Chamilly, tel: 03 85 87 22 24). There's an alternative way back to Mercurey via a large former monastic vineyard, the Domaine d'Aubigny.

Around Mercurey
Near Mercurey, on the D981, the main north-south road of the Côte Chalonnaise, is the Château de Germolles – the only extant palace of the Valois dukes of Burgundy. Philippe le Hardi (1363–1494) bought an existing castle and had leading artists of the day transform it into an occasional home for his wife Marguerite de Flandres. It is open all day in July and August (tel: 03 85 45 10 55).

Just before Germolles, going south, a right turn on the D48 leads to Mellecey and the Vallée des Vaux, with the little wine villages, on the slopes above the river Orbise, of St-Mard-de-Vaux, St Jean-de-Vaux and St-Denis de Vaux. The wines aren't expensive. Try Domaine Michel Isaie (chemin de l'Ouche, 71640 St-Jean-de-Vaux, tel: 03 85 45 23).

Chalon-sur-Saône: a hive of industry
This is Burgundy's second biggest town, and its position on a large navigable river – the Saône, which joins the Rhône at Lyon – has meant that Chalon has always thrived. Its prosperity grew in the nineteenth century, when the Schneider steel business was established at Le Creusot – easily reached by the Canal du Centre, which here joins the Saône. The combination of local steel and navigable waterways attracted shipbuilders, and in the nineteenth century Chalon was a world leader in the construction of military submersibles. To this day, general industry – light engineering, chemicals, glassworks – is economically much more important to Chalon than links with the vineyards that bear its name. There is a medieval quarter, with narrow, pedestrianised streets, old houses, and a cathedral dedicated to St Vincent: medieval but with an early nineteenth-century

GROWERS IN MERCUREY

Domaine Brintet
105 Grande Rue
71640 Mercurey
Tel: 03 85 45 14 50 *(F3)*
This domaine comes highly recommended.

Domaine de la Croix Jacquelet
Grande Rue
Tel: 03 85 45 14 72 *(F3)*
Owned by Faiveley.

Domaine Michel Juillot
59 Grande Rue
71640 Mercurey
Tel: 03 85 98 99 89 *(F3)*
Near-perfect Mercurey, which costs a little more than you usually pay.

Domaine Bruno Lorenzon
14 rue du Reu
71640 Mercurey
Tel:03 85 45 13 51 *(F3)*
Highly recommended.

Domaine de Meix-Foulot
Clos du Château de Montaigu
71640 Mercurey
Tel: 03 85 45 13 92 *(F3)*
Wines are more "rustic" than Juillot's, but in a good way.

Domaine Maurice Protheau
Château d'Etroyes
71640 Mercurey
Tel: 03 85 45 10 84 *(F3)*
Highly recommended.

Domaine François Raquillet
19 rue de Jamproyes
71640 Mercurey
Tel: 03 85 45 14 61 *(F3)*
Opulent wines.

Antonin Rodet
Grande Rue, 71640 Mercurey
Tel: 03 85 98 12 12*(F3)*
Owns the Domaine de Château de Chamiery.

PRICES: moderate

façade. I find old Chalon all the more attractive for being a diverse and thriving town.

Chalon night-life
Chalon has more in the way of nightlife than, er, Beaune or Chablis. There are usually live bands at l'Abattoir (which actually is an old slaughterhouse: 52 quai Saint Cosme, 71100 Chalon-sur-Saône, tel: 03 85 90 94 70).

Shopping for wine
Wine is chiefly represented here at the odd chalet-style Maison des Vins de la Côte Chalonnaise (2 promenade Ste Marie, 71100 Chalon-sur-Saône, tel: 03 85 41 64 00). Here, for a nominal sum, you can taste your way through a large number of local wines. There is also a vast Carrefour supermarket in the Centre Commercial on the left bank of the Saône (tel: 03 85 42 64 00). It's a cliché to say that French supermarkets don't have good wine, but often an untrue one. Many good local growers are represented here – as they often are at village Casinos and Maximarchés.

Caught on film
You'll see signs telling you that this is the cradle of photography ("*le berceau de la photographie*"). So, visit the Musée Nicéphore-Niepce (28 quai des Messageries, 71100 Chalon-sur-Saône, tel: 03 85 41 98, www.museeniepce.com), with its collections of early equipment and photographs – including many historic images of wine and winemaking – and mementos of the local inventor after whom the museum is named who, in 1816, made the first, fugitive photographic images, using a lens and silver salts known to blacken in daylight.

Dambusters
Other signs in Chalon refer to a grimmer recent past – to those who fell "*lachement assassiné par les hordes Teutonnes*" ("cowardly assassinated by the Teutonic hordes"). The town was divided by the line that separated Occupied and Vichy France from 1940–43. Chalon's Resistance gave the British the information for a successful air raid on the dams at Gigny, which lowered the water level in the Saône and reduced its value as a waterway. Then a full-blown insurgency started in February 1942, in the teeth of German countermeasures, not least from the Gestapo, whose interrogation and torture facilities were based in the Place des Halles. This history was celebrated by an exhibition, entitled "Chalon Occupé, Chalon Liberé", on the fiftieth anniversary of the Liberation. More local history is available from L'Espace Patrimoine 24 (quai des Messageries, 71100 Chalon-sur-Saône, tel: 03 85 93 15 98).

Enlightened and musical Givry

Givry's Age of Enlightenment character, with its eighteenth-century town hall built over a gateway, its "Halle Ronde", a round granary building, and its octagonal church, mark it out from many neighbouring medieval villages. At first glance the story of Givry's wine looks as if it comes from the Côte Chalonnaise choir sheet: the "*vin preferé de Henri IV*" ("Henri IV's preferred wine"), with vineyard soils and exposition "identical to Gevrey-Chambertin", apparently.

But, there's more to it. For many years this town's excellent red wines were largely bought in bulk by the Beaune merchants as blending material; then, during the 1980s, the growers took a collective plunge into direct sales. "This is simply the best village of the Côte Chalonnaise," enthuses Givry's leading grower Jean-Marc Joblot. "Nowhere else has the same atmosphere or the same team spirit."

One of the best ways to appreciate this is at the annual *vignerons'* festival called Musicaves, which takes place at the end of June, and which involves food, wine and music. (Enquiries and reservations – which are necessary, given the level of interest – are made by contacting 03 85 98 96 16.)

The Voie Verte

During the 1990s the railway branch-line, which linked Chalon-sur-Saône, Chagny, Cluny, and Mâcon, was grassed over and turned into a cycle route. Givry is the northern point of the stretch that runs without a break to Cluny, 40km (25 miles) south. Most locals would rather have their trains back and it can be rather a boring route at times – a landscape that's fascinating at train speed can be less so on a bike. However, the Voie Verte (the Green Way) does link some fairly far-flung wine villages, and cycles and wine do go well together (no breathalyser, enhanced tasting skills, and instant bonding with any *vélo*-mad proprietors).

St Désert and Bissey-sous-Cruchaud

St Désert is a pretty, unvisited village with a fortified fourteenth-century church. The wines are only entitled to call themselves Côte Chalonnaise, but Domaine Goubard (rue Bassevelle, 71390 St Désert, tel: 03

BELOW *Givry's late-eighteenth-century town hall is built around a monumental gate.*

GROWERS IN GIVRY

Domaine du Clos Salomon
16 rue du clos Salomon
71640 Givry
Tel: 03 85 44 32 24 *(D3)*
Clos Salomon is a
monopole vineyard in
single ownership. Solid,
complex wines for
keeping.

Domaine Joblot
4 rue Pasteur
71640 Givry
Tel: 03 85 44 30 77 *(D3)*
Full-on, oaky red wines;
but the whites here are
also worth looking at.

François Lumpp
36 avenue de Mortières
71640 Givry
Tel: 03 85 44 45 57 *(D3)*
A leader in Givry.

Jean-Paul Ragot
4 rue de l'Ecole
71640 Givry
Tel: 03 85 44 35 67 *(D3)*
First-rate domaine.

Chofflet-Valdenaire Russilly
71640 Russilly
Tel: 03 85 44 34 78 *(D3)*
A couple of kms out of
town to the west, via
a tiny scenic road.

**Michel Sarrazin et Fils
Charnailles**
71640 Jambles
Tel: 03 85 44 30 57 *(D3)*
Burgundy's vineyards have
famously colourful names –
few more so than the Clos
de la Putin – a sound-alike
for "the whore's vineyard"
– "whore" is "putain" –
owned by the Sarrazin
family. Their wines are
definitely worth a detour to
Jambles, 4km (2.5 miles)
west of the town.

PRICES: inexpensive

85 47 91 06), has put the village on the map, especially with good-value lightish red from the slopes of Mont Avril. Goubard also has some well-made Givry, also a bargain.

Like St Désert, Bissey-sous-Cruchaud means a deviation from the north-south route, but it's worth it to call on Christophe Denizot (14 rue des Moirots, 71390 Bissey-sous-Cruchaud, tel: 03 85 92 16 93), who makes a range of inexpensive wines according to the classic, labour-intensive formulae (ploughing, and so on). All his wines, from the Montagny to the Givry and the *crémant*, are good, and some are very good.

Bissey also has a co-op which I feel deserves at least two cheers just for keeping its independence from the local colossus, the Cave de Buxy. This co-op always makes good *crémant*.

Cooperative Buxy

Buxy's cooperative (rue de la Gare, 71390 Buxy, tel: 03 85 92 03 03, and shop: 03 85 92 04 30) put this village on the map; it's thanks to the work of Roger Rageot, its long-time director, that you find the local white appellation, Montagny, on so many British supermarket shelves. Rageot's most important insight was that customers would demand oak maturation, at a time when some in the industry thought it was irrelevant and old-fashioned. Buxy has equally imaginatively seen the potential of big oak *foudres*, and has found a way to mechanise the peasant technique of *pigeage*, or foot-treading. On the marketing side, Buxy has got together with its counterparts in the Auxerrois, at Chablis, and Bailly, to create what they hope will be a world-scale brand in "Blason de Bourgogne". So far economics still mean machine-harvesting and big-batch production – but the latest techniques, to put virtually unfiltered wines on the market, are typically imaginative. There's a *caveau* for tasting.

The old town of Buxy huddles defensively on the high ground, and is worth a look. There's a Musée du Vigneron; details from the tourist office (place de la Gare, tel: 03 85 92 00 16.)

At Marcilly-lès-Buxy, 10km (6 miles) west on the D977, there's an award-winning organic honey producer worth a visit – Dominique Savoye (Boujolles, 71390 Marcilly-lès-Buxy, tel: 03 85 96 10 68).

About 3km (2 miles) before Marcilly, a right turn brings you to Sassangy and its château which, for the last few years, has been the centre of operations for Jean Musso, previously of Dracy-lès-Couches (tel: 03 85 96 18 61). Musso is a kind of refugeee from the appellation system – he sells his Couches wines as simple Bourgogne, refusing the new Côte du Couchois appellation. Musso is organic, a large-scale producer with 25ha and supermarkets as his customers. He partly machine harvests. My tips are his Passe-Tout-Grains for €5 – the only version of this Gamay–Pinot blend I'd ever recommend – and his Hautes-Côtes de Beaune, from the Maranges area.

Montagny

The most famous white appellation of the Côte Chalonnaise is a nice enough little village, which shares the slopes with its vineyards. The village *caveau* has closed, at least for the time being. The excellence of the best grower, Aladame (*see right*), overshadows the rest. Otherwise stalwarts include Alain Roy's Château de Saule, which you see as you approach the village (tel: 03 85 92 11 83) and, in Buxy beside the D961, Château de Cary Potet (tel: 03 85 92 14 48).

Culles-les-Roches

In this village the long geological fault that brings the high plain tumbling into the valley of the Saône takes the form of dramatic limestone cliffs. A scramble up a path from the centre of the village brings you to a cave used as a ready-made Neolithic home. A road leads down through the houses to the former railway station. Beside it is a winery which has recently changed hands, and is changing its name from Domaine Dionysos to Domaine Le Gregoire. It has had some good Montagny in the past – worth a visit to see how things are developing (tel: 03 85 44 01 90).

Where to stay

For the north of the Côte Chalonnaise, Chagny is a good base: see recommendations in the last chapter. In Mercurey, consider the Hostellerie du Val d'Or (*see box, p.104*) around €100 a room. In Chalon, the St-Georges, near the station is a good choice, medium to dear; rather cheaper is the St Jean, overlooking the Saône. Buxy has two good hotels, the cheaper Relais du Montagny, and the grander Hôtel Fontaine de Baranges which also, as it happens, hires out bikes. Finally in St Boil (p.99, A4), the mid-priced and attractive Hôtel-Restaurant Le Cheval Blanc.

For eating out options, Le Petit Blanc in Charecey is a small, bustling place 5km (3 miles) west of Mercurey on the D978, while Chalon's best restaurant is the Moulin de Martorey.

ABOVE *Pinot Noir beginning to change colour.*

LEFT *Christophe Denizot's vineyard; he prides himself on ploughing his soil rather than using herbicides.*

GROWERS IN MONTAGNY

Stéphane Aladame
rue du Lavoir
71390 Montagny-les-Buxy
Tel: 03 85 92 06 01 *(B4)*
I want an edginess in Montagny, and these wines have it in spades. Aladame is now looking for a way into the great appellations of the Côte de Beaune – I just hope their gain isn't Montagny's loss.

Domaine des Moirots,
Christophe Denizot
Bizzey-sous-Cruchaud *(C4)*
See main text.

PRICES: inexpensive

The northern Mâconnais, including Viré and Clessé

There is a kind of anarchy here. Most of Burgundy is classified according to an elaborate and hierarchical system. But, in the Mâconnais, which makes more wine than the Côte d'Or and the Côte Chalonnaise put together, there are no *grand* or *premier cru* vineyards. Instead, there's a free-for-all of forty-three different villages – from Mâcon-Azé through to Mâcon-Vinzelles. What's more, the land is not so expensive that you can only become a *vigneron* through inheritance. This region, with its grand, almost mountainous scenery and its rough-and-ready vinous democracy, could be Burgundy's New World.

A question of expectations

In the north of the Mâconnais producers haven't historically been expected to do more than make low-cost wine (nearly all of which is white and unoaked) that can carry the burgundy appellation, and sell it to négociants, through the intermediary of their local cooperative.

BELOW *In Clessé, the church is eleventh century, with later polycrhomatic roof tiles.*

The potential here may not be quite that of the Côte d'Or: many vineyards tend to be situated at higher altitudes. I find that most white burgundy from this region is a bit thin, though modern winemaking can give it some sort of surface appeal with sweet and floral aromas. There is a handful of growers who are interesting.

Travelling around

While travelling in the Côte d'Or the challenge is to break the monotony of driving up and down the N74. The Mâconnais' convoluted geography, by contrast, makes it impossible to line villages up neatly, so I'll apologise straightaway for sending you in ever-decreasing circles. Just think of it as a change from monotony.

Here we start near the indistinct border with the Côte Chalonnaise at Genouilly and head for Tournus via St-Gengoux-le-National, with slight deviations to visit Cormatin, Brancion and Mancey. We then head down to the villages of the Viré-Clessé appellation, across to Cluny via Igé, and back up the valley of the Grosne to another cluster of wine villages including Cruzille, Lugny, and Azé (*see* map, right).

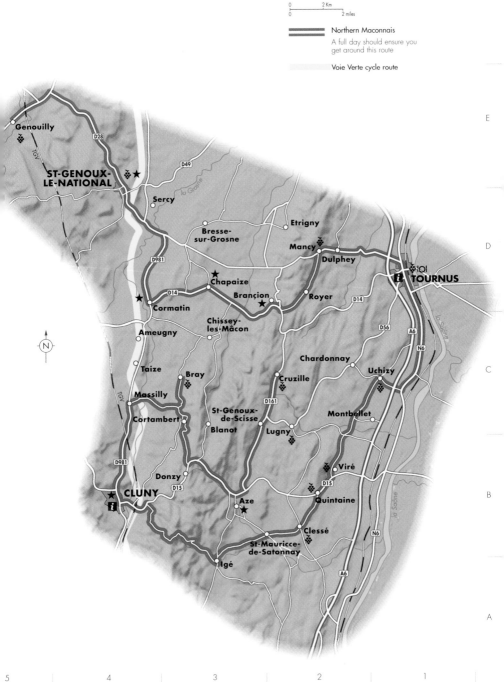

0   2 Km
0   2 miles

Northern Maconnais
A full day should ensure you
get around this route

Voie Verte cycle route

E

Genouilly

D28

TGV

ST-GENOUX-
LE-NATIONAL

D49

Sercy

la Grosne

D

Etrigny

Bresse-
sur-Grosne

Mancy

Dulphey

D981

TOURNUS

Chapaize

Brançion

Royer

D14

Cormatin

D14

la Saône

Chissey-
les-Mâcon

D56

A6

Ameugny

N6

N

Chardonnay

Taize

Cruzille

Uchizy

Bray

C

Massilly

St-Génoux-
de-Scisse

D161

Montbellet

Cortambert

Blanot

Lugny

TGV

D981

Viré

Donzy

D15

D15

CLUNY

Aze

Quintaine

B

Clessé

St-Mauricce-
de-Satonnay

N6

Igé

A6

A

5   4   3   2   1

CLAUDE BROSSE 1656–1731

Southern Burgundy's vineyards, like those of the Côte d'Or, were **enclosed and developed by monks**. But their countrywide reputation is associated with **the story of Claude Brosse**, an unusually tall merchant from **Charnay-lès-Macon**. Brosse is supposed to have put **two casks on a bullock cart** and driven it north for thirty-three days **to the court of Louis XIV**, at Versailles, outside Paris. There he attended mass at the royal chapel. When the congregation knelt, the Sun King was astonished to see one man, Brosse, apparently still standing.
An attendant was **sent to deal with the incident**, who returned to report "Sire, he is kneeling". Having attracted the king's attention, Brosse **offered a tasting**. Louis was impressed, and found the **Mâconnais wine better than that from the Auxerrois** (see p.50) which was then served at court.

Cooperative country

Genouilly is divided both by the river Guye and the main Paris-Marseille TGV line, which thunders past the wine cooperative. This, though smallish (it has eighty members), has an increasing number of fans and is a place to stock up on inexpensive appellations (Cave des Vignerons de la Région de Genouilly, quartier de la Gare, 71460 Genouilly, tel: 03 85 49 23 72).

St-Gengoux-le-National is a wine town, but one where virtually all the growers are members of the Buxy cooperative. There's a village *caveau* (Cave de St-Gengoux-le-National, rue Longemeau, 71460 St-Gengoux-le-National, tel: 03 85 92 61 75), selling the local Mâcon Rouge and also separately vinified *cuvées* from such little-known *lieux-dits* as Savigny-sur-Grosne, a kilometre or two away. One reason to stroll in the medieval streets is to visit the exceptional chocolatier who used to work for Lameloise (see p.97). He is Jean-Pierre Demortière (rue de la Commerce, tel: 03 85 92 60 86). But, don't try to drive his creations home through France except in cool weather.

Cormatin: visit the château

There are few wine-growers on the inland valley of the river Grosne; the reason to stop at Cormatin is to visit the château, and in particular the private rooms of the Marquis Jacques du Blé and his wife Claude Phélipeaux, which have kept their original elaborately painted panelling from the 1620s. Note the figure of temperance in the Cabinet de Ste-Cecilia, with a glass of water and a toe swollen by gout, caused perhaps by too much wine-drinking. Visitors are taken round in groups, with some translation for English speakers (tel: 03 85 50 16 55).

If you are in the mood to wander around tiny roads, take the D14 to Chapaize, with a break to admire the pure Romanesque lines of its eleventh-century church. At Brancion, which is dominated by a hillside castle, largely fourteenth-century, take the D182 to Royer and Dulphey, joining the D215 a little beyond Mancey.

Another cooperative

Dulphey is where the small Mancey cooperative makes its wine and there's a small *caveau* here (closed in August; tel: 03 85 51 11 31). Its main tasting and sales area is a further 10km (6 miles) on, 500m from the A6 motorway exit for Tournus, on the left on the Route Nationale 6 going north to Chalon (Cave de Mancey, En Velnoux, 71700 Tournus, tel: 03 85 51 00 83). This small co-op also co-ordinates a marketing group called De Vigne en Verre, so at Tournus you can taste quite a wide range including Côte d'Or producers. Mancey is best known for its good and cheap old-vine Mâcon Rouge.

RIGHT *Even here in the Mâconnais, where the wines rarely cost more than €8, growers stick with traditional high-maintenance, high-density planting.*

Fleeing Norsemen in Tournus

The river Saône washes three towns on its right bank as it passes through southern Burgundy – Tournus is the smallest of the three, but architecturally it is easily the most distinguished, because here, unlike in Cluny, a Romanesque abbey-church survived the Revolution intact. Its vaulted stone rooms give a sense of both physical and spiritual security. It was built between 950 and 1120AD by monks bearing the bones of their patron saint, St Philibert, and fleeing Norse raiders on France's Atlantic coast.

Opposite St Philibert is a *caveau* in an old building. It looks like a tourist trap, but in fact this is the point of sale for one of Burgundy's best young growers: Pascal Pauget (5 rue Fénelon, 71700 Tournus, tel: 03 85 32 53 15). Pauget learned his craft in the Mâconnais, working at the organic Guillot-Broux estate in Cruzille; his vineyards include a holding at Mâcon-Prety which is, I think, the only appellation in Burgundy on the left, or "wrong" bank of the Saône. His Mâcon Rouge isn't quite as cheap as the Mancey co-op's but his wines are individual and they are certainly incredible value.

Viré and Clessé

These two villages have given give their name to the recently created Viré-Clessé appellation – which is intended to recognize that this sub-region is a notch or two above all the other Mâcon-Villages appellations.

Most of the members of the Viré cooperative qualify, although this area's most famous producer, Jean Thévenet, doesn't, and there's some consequent cynicism about its value, beyond making the co-op's wines look rather grander than they did before.

LOCAL INFORMATION

Office de Tourisme
avenue de la Promenade
71460 St-Gengoux-le-National
Tel: 03 85 92 52 05

Office de Tourisme
place Carnot
71700 Tournus
Tel: 03 85 27 00 20

Information Kiosk
place de l'Abbaye
71700 Tournus
Tel: 03 85 32 59 44

Office de Tourisme
rue Mercière
71250 Cluny
Tel: 03 85 59 05 34
www.perso.wanadoo.fr/otcluny

BIKE HIRE AND ELECTRIC "TROTTINETTES":
Samui-Loisires
Gare SNCF
71460 St-Gengoux
Tel: 03 85 92 56 48

ABOVE *The surviving original wing of Cormatin's astonishing renaissance château.*

RIGHT *The pleasures of "la chasse" tempt many growers.*

Thévenet and Guillemot-Michel: the odd ones out

Thévenet's Domaine de la Bongran in Quintaine is disqualified from the new Viré-Clessé appellation because his grapes have too high sugar levels after fermentation. From the sweet wine, which often shows the effects of botrytis, the "noble rot" of Sauternes and elsewhere, through to the nearly dry, these wines are unusual and distinguished.

Thévenet's neighbours in Quintaine are Marc and Pierrette Guillemot-Michel, who work Biodynamically. Their Chardonnay vines, like Thévenet's, include some Chardonnay Musqué, which has a perfumed, Muscat-like character. They are very concentrated wines, for me perhaps even sometimes too much so.

Another small and convoluted road gets us to Cluny via Igé – where we can call on Domaine Fichet (see right) which got under way, as so often the case in the Mâconnais, by pulling out of the local co-op and going it alone.

Benedictine Cluny

In 910AD, Count William of Auvergne handed over not just the town of Cluny, but also its serfs, vines and meadows, to Benedictine monks. William wrote: "Although I myself am unable to despise all things, nevertheless by receiving despisers of this world, whom I believe to be righteous, I may receive the reward of the righteous."

The result was a structured and hierarchical development of monasticism, from which the Cistercian order soon emerged as a separate strain. The third monastery church here, built and consecrated in 1132, was the largest church in Europe until

St Peter's in Rome was rebuilt in the sixteenth century. Most of it was demolished for building material during the Revolution, although a surviving transept gives a sense of its scale, and the early twelfth-century frescos at Berzé-la-Ville (see p.118) show how the vast interiors would have been decorated.

Bray and Cruzille

The Bray vineyards are isolated, even by Mâconnais standards, but it's quite easy to find the appellation's top name, Henri Lafarge of the Domaine de la Combe (tel: 0385 50 02 18, http://perso.wanadoo.fr/henri.lafarge). Lafarge is justifiably pleased with his Pinot Noir and his barrique-fermented Bourgogne Blanc, but the red and white Mâcon Villages steal the limelight.

Then on to Cruzille: the name behind the Cruzille appellation is Pierre Guillot, who in 1954 made France's first-ever organic wine in this village. His health had suffered from his imprisonment as a POW and he found he had become intolerant of sulphur. Today, his skilled grandson Julien is one of the few who can make successful no-sulphur wines. (Domaine des Vignes du Mayne, Sagy-le-Haut, 71260 Cruzille-en-Mâconnais, tel: 03 85 33 20 15, www.vignes-du-maynes.com.)

Pierre's other son Jean-Gérard gave up on no-sulphur, but his estate remains organic and makes successful wines (Domaine Guillot-Broux, Le Bourg, 71260 Cruzille-en-Mâconnais, tel: 03 85 33 29 74). Jean-Gérard's son Emmanuel recently planted some Chardonnay en foule – the style of mass-planting used in France before the nineteenth-century phylloxera epidemic. Neither estate is rock-bottom cheap.

Name-swapping in Lugny

There's a proposal to simplify the Mâconnais's appellation system by abolishing the name of Cruzille on wine labels and substituting that of Lugny, better known because of its much-improved cooperative – Cave Cooperative de Lugny (tel: 03 85 33 22 85, www.cave-lugny.com).

The village has one independent grower (he's organic, he picks by hand, uses natural yeasts and so on): Hubert Laferrère of the Domaine St Denis (Bourg, 71260 Lugny, tel: 03 85 33 24 33). Like many of the top names of the Mâconnais, Laferrère strongly believes in late harvesting for concentrated flavours.

The caves of Azé

There's a wine co-op here, but you shouldn't leave the region without exploring at least one of the limestone caves. Blanot has vast spaces and sheer descents, but Azé scores with its endlessly dripping pool with small crustacea adapted to their lightless underground world (tel: 03 85 33 32 23).

The southern Mâconnais, including Pouilly, Fuissé, and Vinzelles

T he Mâconnais used to be divided between the north and Pouilly-Fuissé. Though not formally classified as *premiers crus*, the vineyards under the crags of Solutré and Vergisson were considered the nearest southern Burgundy got to matching the Côte d'Or.

Pouilly or not Pouilly?

Over the past two decades some influential newcomers have settled in the South, but in general, outside the villages with the prefix of "Pouilly". Pouilly-Fuissé is long established – the appellation was granted as early as 1936 – and the name commands a price premium, particularly in the United States. The New Wave, however, has put as much energy into simple Mâcon-Villages.

But Pouilly-Fuissé, with the rarer Pouilly-Loché and Pouilly-Vinzelles, does set the tone for the southern Mâconnais, partly because it comes from such an extraordinary place. The peaks of Solutré, Vergisson, and Mont de Pouilly were underwater calcareous sea reefs. Then, when the earth moved and created the Côte d'Or, these reared up on their sides, like the prows of sinking ships.

Travelling around

BELOW *The rock of Solutré, a key archeological site, where evidence of the slaughter of thousands of prehistoric beasts has been found (see p.119).*

This route starts just outside Mâcon, in Charney, then takes us up the valley of the Petit Gronse – the so-called Val Lamartinien, where places like La Roche Vineuse, Milly, and Sologny are prominent in the Mâconnais revival. We make a detour to view the extraordinary sights of the two villages called Berzé, and we end up on the northern borders with the Pays Beaujolais, reached via the peaks of Vergisson and Solutré, the scene of interesting archeological finds.

Dozy Mâcon

Mâcon has the reputation of a smug little town populated by administrators. Its attractions include a lovely eighteenth-century bridge and some great restaurants (I once found myself at a table next to Jack Lang, the former culture minister and archetypal Champagne socialist). It might remind you of Chalon, but it's sleepier and the look of the place is a little more southern (the chief signifier for me is the angle of the roofs, which become flatter where winter snow is not a design issue).

Each spring Mâcon's exhibition centre holds one of France's leading wine trade fairs. Yet despite being the capital of Burgundy's most productive wine area, there are no major-league shippers currently based here.

Mâcon does have a well-run Maison des Vins (484 avenue De-Lattre-de-Tassigny, tel: 03 85 22 91 11, www.maison-des-vins.com), which unlike its counterpart in Chalon offers a wide range of Burgundy appellations – it doesn't just focus on its home region.

Charnay-lès-Mâcon

If you believe the legend of Claude Brosse (see p.110) this is where Mâcon's wine trade took off, so perhaps it's appropriate to call in on a small négociant. Trenel is equally at home in Beaujolais, w h i c h

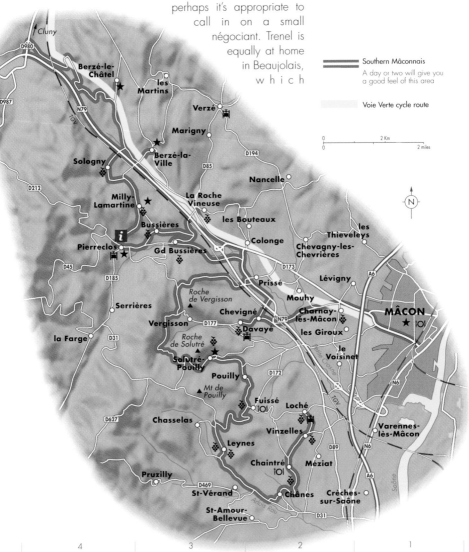

Southern Mâconnais
A day or two will give you a good feel of this area

Voie Verte cycle route

ABOVE *Spring flowers beside Dominique Lafon's new vineyards in Milly-Lamartine.*

RIGHT *A frescoed Judgement in the chapel at Berzé-la-Ville.*

supplies its red wines, apart from an earthy Mâcon Rouge, and in its white Mâcon and Pouilly appellations. This is the old-fashioned face of this region, at its best (Maison Trenel, 33 chemin du Buery-le-Voisinet, 71850 Charnay-lès-Mâcon, tel: 03 85 34 48 20).

Davayé
Davayé is one of the villages included in this region's odd catch-all appellation, St-Véran (see p.120), which includes vineyards both north and south of the landmark appellation of Pouilly-Fuissé. It's the home of the Lycée Viticole; growers in southern Burgundy generally study here rather than in Beaune. As at Beaune, you can visit, taste and buy by appointment (Lycée-Viticole de Mâcon-Davayé, Domaine des Poncetys, 71960 Davayé, tel: 03 85 33 56 20). Also in Davayé is one of the Mâcon producers you're most likely to find abroad: the prolific Domaine des Deux Rôches (71960 Davayé, tel: 03 85 35 86 51). This domaine machine-harvests.

Prissé
This village is a few more kilometres down the D17 and further into the valley of the Petite Grosne, also known as the Val Lamartinien, in tribute to the Romantic poet and French statesman Alphonse de Lamartine (1790–1869), who was born in Mâcon and grew up in Milly.

La Roche Vineuse – all change
Formerly known as St-Sorlin: its current name dates from after the Revolution. It used to be a railway collection point for Mâcon wines, but the line is now the southern leg of the Voie Verte (see p.105). Since 1987 it's been home to one of the architects of the Mâconnais revival, Olivier Merlin (vers l'Eglise, 71960 La Roche Vineuse, tel: 03 85 36 62 09). Merlin's innovation was to make white Mâcon in barrels, like serious white burgundy; he's also now a local négociant, able to indulge a passion for Beaujolais by making a little Moulin-à-Vent in the classic manner. Merlin makes "tighter" wines than Verget in the village of Sologny; perhaps less crowd-pleasing, but rewarding.

You could make an 8km (5-mile) round trip up the D85 to Verzé to look for the new Leflaive (see p.85) vineyard. But there's no winemaking done there; the grapes will be pressed and the juice taken up to Puligny-Montrachet. It would be more sensible to cross under the TGV line (which visitors admire but the locals don't) to Grand Bussières and Bussières, where there's an eleventh-century Romanesque church and a good grower of both red and white Mâcon: Domaine Jean-Philippe Baptista (Petit Bussières, 71960 Bussières, tel: 03 85 37 77 79). His neighbour Philippe Trebignaud has moved up the road to Milly-Lamartine. But before you go there, make a short detour to the village of Pierreclos.

Pierreclos' spiral stair
The grandfather of the leading grower here, Jean-Claude Thévenet (see box), used to help run the cellars and vineyards of the village's twelfth- to sixteenth-century castle, the imposing Château de Pierreclos. It has the largest spiral staircase of any building in France, and it can be visited between 9.30 and 12.30am, and in the afternoon as well in the high season (tel: 03 85 35 73 73). Don't miss the kitchen, or the displays relating to breadmaking and winemaking.

Milly-Lamartine: flood warning
English-speaking readers tend to know Lamartine, if at all, through Mark Twain's observation that Lamartine was too freely moved to tears. "That man never could come within the influence of a subject in the least pathetic without overflowing his banks. He ought to be dammed – or leveed, I should more properly say." (The Innocents Abroad, 1869). In Milly's rue Principale is the handsome two-storey house (tel: 03 85 37 70 33) that featured in many of Lamartine's writings, and where he would return annually to supervise the vintage.

Dominique Lafon of Meursault (see p.87) bought an 8ha estate in this village in the late 1990s, to which he's now added a further holding in the village of Chardonnay (yes, there really is such a place, and the grape may well take its name from that

GROWERS IN THE SOUTHERN MACONNAIS
. . . .

Domaine Lucien Denuziller
Bourg
71960 Solutré-Pouilly
Tel: 03 85 35 80 77 *(B3)*
Rich wines.

Olivier Larochette
rue du Lavoir
71570 Chaintré
Tel: 03 85 35 61 50 *(A2)*
Dedicated Pouilly-Fuissé producer.

Domaine Manciat-Poncet
65 chemin des Gérards
71850 Charnay-lès-Mâcon
Tel: 03 85 29 22 93 *(B2)*
Hand-picked grapes.

Domaine Alain Normand
chemin de la Grange-du-Dîme
71960 La Roche Vineuse
Tel: 03 85 36 61 69 *(C3)*
Serious, organic, good value.

Domaine Jean-Claude Thévenet et Fils
71960 Pierreclos
Tel: 03 85 35 72 21 *(C4)*
Unrelated to the Thévenets of Quintaine (see p.112).

Lucien Thomas
Domaine de la Feuillarde
71960 Prissé
Tel: 03 85 34 54 45
A top St-Véran. (B/C2/3)

INDEPENDENT GROWERS IN LOCHE:
Domaine Alain Delaye
Les Mûres
71000 Loché
Tel: 03 85 35 61 63 *(B2)*

Domaine C. et L. Tripoz
71000 Loché
Tel: 03 85 35 66 09 *(B2)*

PRICES: inexpensive to moderate

ABOVE *The sunny south. The Mâconnais enjoys an average of sixty hours more sunshine each year than the Côte d'Or.*

of the village) to the north. No visiting, but you can buy the wines in Meursault, and in Milly there's always the excellent Philippe Trebignaud with his Domaine de la Sarazinière (Verchères, Milly-Lamartine, tel: 03 85 37 76 04).

Sologny
This village is the headquarters of Maison Verget, one of the biggest white burgundy names to have appeared in recent years. Its Belgian owner, Jean-Marie Guffens, started out working in the often overlooked Mâconnais appellations before using this base to take the Côte d'Or and even Chablis by storm. He believes in making "real" wines: hand-picked but designed for pleasure – plenty of lees-stirring, for example – and should you find him in full flow you will be informed and entertained (Le Bourg, 71960 Sologny, tel: 03 85 51 66 00, www.verget-sa.com).

The frescoes of Berzé-la-Ville
In 1887, a priest discovered frescos here, and they were soon identified as belonging to the same period as the great eleventh-century abbey of Cluny. Through being hidden under plaster their bright colours had kept much of their freshness. It's called La Chapelle aux Moines and it's unmissable (71960

LOCHE: THE FORGOTTEN POUILLY

The town of **Loché is the site of Mâcon's TGV station**. The appellation of Pouilly-Loché is little more than half the size of Pouilly-Vinzelles and is **dominated by the négociant Louis Jadot,** which buys and vinifies the crop of Château de Loché (tel: 03 85 35 61 38).

Berzé-la-Ville – unfortunately, there's no telephone number).

Four-and-a-half kilometres (2.8 miles) away is one of Burgundy's oldest military castles (the oldest parts are ninth-century) dominating the southern approach to Cluny. Château de Berzy-le-Chatel (tel: 03 85 36 60 83).

The recommended route now involves going on towards Cluny, then picking up the expressway, the N79, and taking it back to the La Roche Vineuse exit, then turning right and right again to find the road to Vergisson.

Vergisson

The sloping, stony vineyards under the prow of the rock of Vergisson make this an important wine village in the Pouilly-Fuissé and Mâcon-Vergisson appellations. The Bureau Interprofessionel's directory lists no fewer than forty-six growers; ten more than Chassagne-Montrachet. Most of them belong to the local cooperative, the Cave Coopérative des Grands Crus Blancs (100 Terres Neyme, 71680 Vinzelles, tel: 03 85 27 05 77/03 85 27 05 70).

Solutré-Pouilly

The rock of Solutré, looking rather like a refugee from Utah's Monument Valley, proved in 1866 to have, at its foot, the bones of around 100,000 bison, deer, and mammoths. They were slaughtered over a period stretching roughly from 30,000–10,000BC – not, as was at one time thought, by driving them up and over the cliff, but by ambushing the beasts as they passed this landmark in the course of their seasonal migrations. For more information, the Musée Départemental de Préhistorie is within the rock near the car park (tel: 03 85 35 85 24.) The rock itself is quite a gentle climb – allow forty-five minutes for the round trip.

Picturesque Leynes

In this village, once a stopping point on the pilgrim route to Compostela (see p.56) we're on the frontier with Beaujolais, and again in St-Véran. This is a confusing appellation. It's not a real place; there is a village in the appellation called St-Vérand,

WHERE TO STAY AND EAT

STAYING OUT OF TOWN:
Château de la Barge
71680 Crêches-sur-Saône
Tel: 03 85 23 93 23
Affordable.

Château des Poccards
120 route des Poccards
71870 Huringey
Tel: 03 85 32 08 27
Magnificent. Huringey
is north of Lévigny.

EATING IN TOWN:
Restaurant Pierre
7 rue Dufour
Tel: 03 85 38 14 23
Top notch; and it has
a bistro baby brother...

Au P'tit Pierre
10 rue Gambetta
Tel: 03 85 39 48 84

Le St Laurent
1 quai Bouchacourt
Tel: 03 85 39 29 19
Very good, and just over
the bridge.

EATING OUT OF TOWN:
Au Pouilly-Fuissé
71960 Fuissé
Tel: 03 85 35 60 68

La Table de Chaintré
71960 Fuissé
Tel: 03 85 32 90 95

but the "d" is left out of the appellation name so as not to cause confusion with another village, also called St-Vérand, which is in southern Beaujolais. St-Véran covers a large and diverse area; the clay soils of the southern village wines give them a livelier quality than Davayé and Prissé, with their greater limestone content.

Until 1971, when the new name was dreamed up, Leynes, and the other villages entitled to the appellation, sold their white wine as Beaujolais Blanc. The biggest name in Leynes doesn't make a particular speciality of St-Véran, though he can be expected to have one or two examples. This is Jean Rijckaert (pronounced "ray-cart"), until recently Jean-Marie Guffens' partner in Verget, and now a négociant and vineyard owner in his own right. Same broad, rich style (En Correaux, 71570 Leynes, tel: 03 85 35 15 09). Otherwise Château des Correaux, the former Château de Leynes, run by Jean Bernard (71570 Leynes, tel: 03 85 35 11 59).

Vinzelles

Until recently there wouldn't have been much to say about Vinzelles. Like Loché, this village succeeded in getting a Pouilly-hypenated appellation for its powerfully-flavoured wines, but there's so little of it – with just 54ha it's about the size of a single major Bordeaux estate. But in 2000 Jean-Philippe and Jean-Guillaume Bret, fresh from work experience in California and with Dominique Lafon (see p.87), took their 4ha family domaine out of the cooperative, began farming it organically, and soon after started a négociant business. The brothers, often mistaken for twins, are very serious and very nice, and you'd think the only drawback would be the price. But it isn't – particularly for the Mâcon-Villages they make from bought-in grapes (Domaine de la Soufrandière, 71680 Vinzelles, tel: 03 85 35 67 72).

Chaintré

From the Brets' vineyard in Vinzelles, overlooking the plain of the Saône, you can look into the next appellation and the vineyard of their neighbour Gérard Valette, a fellow pillar of Les

Artisans Vignerons de Bourgogne du Sud, a new association of the region's more ambitious producers. He is an admirer of Jules Chauvet (see p.122) and an individualist who bottles his top wine, the Pouilly-Fuissé Clos de Monsieur Noly, after what some regard as an outrageously long time in cask. The inexpensive appellations are excellent and affordable too (Domaine Valette, Verchères, 71570 Chaintré, tel: 03 85 35 62 97).

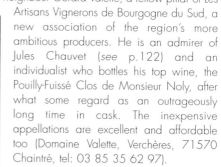

Beaujolais: the *cru* villages

Good Beaujolais is tragically cheap. It comes from a region that, like Germany or Lambrusco, boomed in the second half of the twentieth century, only to suffer for the very qualities that created its success. For some, Beaujolais is less of a real wine than, say, Australian Chardonnay. But whereas a big-selling Australian wine will be made in a winery that looks like an oil refinery, Beaujolais Nouveau comes from the small vats of countless peasant farmers. Beaujolais is not an industrial wine – it's just trying to look "modern" in a rather old-fashioned way.

Not quite what it was

Now, Beaujolais is a place that's seen better days – like Cuba, or an English seaside resort. Beaujolais producers often boast of *vielles vignes*; what they sometimes mean is that their income doesn't allow them to replace decrepit vines. A significant number will be dead, and the others overcropped to make up the shortfall.

But, Beaujolais still has a guaranteed market on its doorstep in France's second city, Lyon. It also offers inexpensive mature wine – try visiting an old-fashioned merchant like Ferraud in Belleville to discover five-year-old *cru* Beaujolais – for the price of an anonymous New World branded wine.

Travelling around (*see* map p.123)

This itinerary of the best villages (there are no officially recognised single vineyards) begins in St-Amour-Bellevue – in the area that has a kind of dual nationality with Burgundy – then visits Juliénas, Chénas, La Chapelle-de-Guinachay, Romanèche-Thorins, Fleurie, Chiroubles, Villié-Morgon, Régnié-Durette, St-Lager, and the Brouilly and Côte de Brouilly appellations, Belleville and St-Jean d'Ardières, and ends up at the château-winemaker-hotel of Pizay, where you might consider staying after totting up the savings you've made with your inexpensive wine-buying.

St-Amour-Bellevue: what's in a name?

The church here (twelfth-century, restored in the nineteenth century) contains the relics of St Amor, the converted Roman legionary who gives the

LEFT *It's not just the vines that enjoy the extra warmth of the Mâconnais.*

BELOW *Grapes and gropes: a roundabout expression of the spirit of Clochemerle.*

GROWERS IN
ST-AMOUR AND JULIENAS

Domaine de l'Ancien Relais
Marie-Hélène Poitevin/
Jean-Yves Miday
Les Chamonards
71570 St-Amour-Bellevue
Tel: 03 85 37 16 05 *(E2)*
See main text.

Domaine Denis et
Hélène Barbelet
Les Billards
71570 St-Amour Bellevue
Tel: 03 85 36 51 36 *(E2)*
St-Amour made to keep.

Domaine Chataigner-
Durand
Jean-Marc Monnet
La Ville, 69840 Juliénas
Tel: 04 74 04 45 46 *(E2)*
Rich, powerful wines.

Domaine des Duc
71570 St-Amour-Bellevue
Tel: 03 85 37 10 08 *(E2)*
Good unoaked Fleurie.

Château de Juliénas
69840 Juliénas
Tel: 04 74 04 41 43 *(E2)*
www.chateaudejulienas.com
See main text.

Domaine Lilian et
Sandrine Matray
Paquelet, 69840 Juliénas
Tel: 04 74 04 45 57 *(E2)*
Serious Beaujolais.

Laurent Perrachon
Domaine des Mouilles
69840 Juliénas
Tel: 04 74 04 40 44 *(E2)*
An old Juliénas family.

Michel Tête
Domaine du Clos du Fief
Les Gonnards
69840 Juliénas
Tel: 04 74 04 41 62 *(E2)*
The other big name in the
village; big wines.

PRICES: inexpensive

village its name, and also St Viator, a fourth-century saint from Lyon, an early centre of Christianity. You might also look in on the village pottery: Le Plâtre Durant (71570 St-Amour, tel: 03 85 37 12 50). Some of St-Amour's wine-growers are felt to take too much advantage of the marketing lift they're given – especially around Valentine's Day – by their village's name.

Juliénas and its château

In Juliénas, the château is both a tourist attraction and a worthwhile wine producer (*see* left). The lord of Beaujeu (*see* p.132) had a castle on this site in the thirteenth century; the present handsome château dates from the early sixteenth century, with some rebuilding in the eighteenth. Today, some of the vineyards are leased to Georges Duboeuf (*see* p.125), and to Jean-Marc Monnet, of Domaine Châteignier-Durand.

A 9km (5.6-mile) drive up the D137 (taking the left fork at the war memorial, past the château) takes you to the mountain village of Cenves, which has a Maison du Fromage, where you can taste and buy local cheeses (tel: 04 74 04 61 23).

Distinguishing the *crus*: Juliénas and St-Amour

Jean-Yves Miday is based in St-Amour, but also has holdings in Juliénas, Fleurie, and a little Beaujolais-Villages in St-Vérand. "It's not easy to spot a St-Amour blind," he says; "I'm not sure I could do it even with my own wines. And they vary – on the higher slopes they're more tannic and take longer to come round. But to generalise, St-Amour is more feminine, Juliénas more masculine. Fleurie is lighter, but completely different from St-Amour: Fleuries taste of blackcurrant whereas St-Amours are like yellow-fleshed peaches, and spicier."

Jules Chauvet (1907–1989)

La Chapelle-de-Guinchay is a village a little bigger than Meursault, and, with Château Bonnet and Hubert Lapierre (*see* p.124) is the base for two of the Beaujolais *crus'* best producers. It owes its place in history to its most famous son, who ran a now-defunct négociant called Chauvet Frères.

It is a paradox that one of the most influential opponents of chemically aided viticulture should have been a researcher and one-time collaborator with the Nobel Prize-winning biochemist Otto Warburg. Jules Chauvet's inquisitiveness took him from fermentation science to food-and-wine matching (with his friend, the Michelin-starred restaurateur Alain Chapel). With oenologist Professor Emile Peynaud, he travelled to Grasse in Provence to learn from fragrance blenders, and subsequently grouped wine aromas into families (floral, fruit, animal, mineral and so on). His dislike of the effects of sulphur in wine has inspired winemakers based in Villié-Morgon; in the Mâconnais Jean Thévenet and

Gérard Valette are among his many admirers. There is now a Rue Jules Chauvet in La Chapelle de Guinchay, "but in his lifetime", observes Thévenet, "they called him an old fool".

Cruising the *crus*
One day, two days, three – the choice is yours. There's plenty to see and do

Moulin-à-Vent: France's first appellation

Moulin-à-Vent, like Morgon, is one of the most serious and long-lasting of the Beaujolais *crus*. The hamlet itself is administratively part of Romanèche-Thorins (some of the appellation is actually within the village limits of Chénas). For the purposes of the appellation, however, Romanèche-Thorins is part of Moulin-à-Vent. It happened this way because of inter-village rivalries: the granitic, manganese-rich, east-facing slopes that lie between the villages of La Chapelle-de-Guinchay, Chénas, and Romanèche had long been regarded

as special. A hamlet with the name of Les Thorins laid a claim to them, to the point of hyphenating its name with that of Romanèche. But then in 1924 an even smaller hamlet named after a windmill went to court to get them – and it succeeded.

A windmill (eighteenth-century, with recently-restored sails) – the windmill, indeed, from which Moulin-à-Vent takes its name – is on the left on the D266 a kilometre from Chénas in the direction of Romanèche-Thorins. Its owners are the proprietors of the Domaine du Moulin-à-Vent (contact Denis Chastel-Sauvet, tel: 03 85 35 58 91), not to be confused with the equally reputable Château du Moulin-à-Vent (tel: 03 85 35 50 68).

Opposite is a *caveau* run by the local growers' union (tel: 03 85 35 58 09, www.moulin-a-vent.net). However, there's only one anonymous wine to taste – selected each year to represent the appellation.

Chénas

Chénas is the smallest, and arguably least well-known of the Beaujolais *crus*. The village lost a certain cachet when its best vineyards were given to Moulin-à-Vent. If you want a taste, go to the neoclassical château where the village's coop is based and whose *caveau* offers tastings (tel: 04 74 04 48 19).

Distinguishing the *crus*: Chénas and Moulin-à-Vent

Hubert Lapierre makes wine in two robust, long-lived appellations: Chénas and Moulin-à-Vent. "The difference between the two is in the structure, not their flavours. When Chénas is young the tannins are angular, a bit rustic. Moulin-à-Vent is rounder, a little less aggressive. They both age well, if anything for longer than Juliénas. They all *"pinotte"* as we say, with time – that's to say that after a few years tasters can mistake them for mature burgundy made from Pinot Noir."

Romanèche-Thorins: railways and wine

Is any other wine region so identified with a single name as Beaujolais is with Georges Duboeuf? Yet the man who gave the world Beaujolais Nouveau only got going on his own in 1964. Critics often take issue with Beaujolais Nouveau's reliance on such techniques as heavy chaptalisation (the addition of sugar during fermentation to raise alcohol levels) and cold fermentation with the 71B yeast strain, which creates intense aromas of red fruit, bananas, even bubblegum, preceded by high-temperature "thermo-vinification", used to leech colour and fruit flavours into the juice. But it wouldn't be fair to blame them all on Duboeuf, who until he opened his new winery was chiefly someone who marketed wines made by growers or cooperatives. His wines are no longer bubble-gummy, and in blind tastings usually equal or outperform the efforts of Beaujolais' best growers.

Duboeuf has taken over the disused railway station in Romanèche-Thorins for his impressive wine museum and railway museum complex, the Hameau du Vin. It bears the mark of his time in California, but isn't tacky or self-promoting. He's also created a series of themed gardens near the site of the new winery, Plaisirs en Beaujolais (tel: 03 85 35 22 22 www.hameauenbeaujolais.com).

Before Georges Duboeuf, Romanèche's wine hero was Benoit Raclet, called the "saviour of the vine" for his discovery in 1844 of a technique to combat the Pyralid moth. His former home is a museum (tel: 03 85 35 55 04) and Raclet is the focus of an annual celebration (involving tasting, naturally) on the last Saturday in October.

Romanèche-Thorins is Maison Jadot of Beaune's centre of operations in the Beaujolais; in 1996 Jadot bought a major estate, the 36ha Château des Jacques, which it's making the flagship for an entirely different approach – Beaujolais as a

FAR LEFT *A 1873 locomotive at the Duboeuf visitors' centre.*

LEFT *Topiary at the Château de Pizay (see p.130).*

RIGHT *A bastion of tradition: Maison Ferraud in Belleville.*

FAR RIGHT *Mediterranean-style roof tiles take the place of slate in Beaujolais.*

GROWERS IN CHIROUBLES

Domaine E. Cheysson
Jean-Pierre Large
Clos des Farges
69115 Chiroubles
Tel: 04 74 04 22 02 *(C3)*
Founded in 1870, a time when Chiroubles was famous for turnips. Cheysson's wine suffer from no lack of concentration despite the altitude.

Domaine de la Combe
aux Loups
Méziat Père et fils
69115 Chiroubles
Tel: 04 74 04 24 02 *(C3)*
Key figures here.

Les Héritiers du Comte
de Raousset
Les Près
69115 Chiroubles
Tel: 04 74 69 16 19 *(C3)*
www.scea-de-raousset.fr
One of the mainstays of the appellation – ripe, concentrated wines.

Sylvain Loron
Domaine de Frédière
69115 Chiroubles
Tel: 04 74 04 23 97 *(C3)*
Vibrant wines.

Gilles Méziat
Domaine du Petit Puits
Le Verdy, 69115 Chiroubles
Tel: 04 74 69 15 90 *(C3)*
He's nephew to Gérard at Domaine la Combe aux Loups (above).

PRICES: inexpensive

"serious" wine, made and cask-aged like a burgundy, without semi-carbonic maceration. There are many growers who think this is the right direction – for example Jean-Paul Brun (*see* p.137). Make up your own mind – and the château is a fine building. Château les Jacques is to be found at Les Jacques, 71570 Romanèche-Thorins (tel: 03 85 35 51 51 64, www.louisjadot.com).

Other attractions
The Musée Guillon du Compagnonnage (La Pierre, 71570 Romanèche-Thorins, tel: 03 85 35 22 02) was created around the life and work of the late nineteenth-century master carpenter Pierre-François Guillon and his apprentices, or *compagnons*. It has all the pleasant randomness of the best provincial museums. Also a minor zoo: Touroparc (tel: 03 85 35 51 53, www.touroparc.com).

Fleurie: everything in the garden's lovely
Fleurie has a name that might have inspired Duboeuf's famous flower labels; the name is said to be one reason that merchants find it the easiest *cru* to sell. Its freshness and drinkability probably also help. Several producers' labels refer to a nineteenth-century chapel of the Madonna overlooking the vineyards: for instance, the delicious wines of Domaine de la Madone, Jean-Marc et Maryse Despres (La Madone, 69820 Fleurie, tel: 04 74 69 81 51).

Chiroubles
This terraced hill village has the most elevated vineyards, the best views and the lightest wines of all the *cru* villages. It is the setting of April's Fête des Crus of young *cru* wines that have just *font leurs Pacques* – celebrated their first Easter – and

so are ready to be tasted. In 1996, the growers here also created Burgundy's and Beaujolais' first all-woman Confrérie, Les Demoiselles de Chiroubles.

From here you could either drive straight to the wine village of Villié-Morgon, or make a detour to Avenas, 7km (4 miles) away (C4). If you do the latter you can enjoy the view from the 660m (2,165 feet) high pass on the D18, "La Terrasse", and see a Romanesque masterpiece of sculpture in the church of Avenas-en-Beaujolais, a twelfth-century white limestone altar featuring an enthroned Christ.

Villié-Morgon

Among this village's famous names some, such as Jean Foillard and Marcel Lapierre at Domaine des Chênes (see p.127) work in a tradition they attribute to Jules Chauvet (see p.122) of vibrant wines made without sulphur. Others, notably Jadot's newly bought Château de Bellevue (tel: 04 74 04 24 37), look to make burgundian-style wines with barrel-ageing. The point of departure is the appellation's soil of decomposed schists – in other words, manganese-rich sand and gravel. The two famous vineyards are the Mont de Py, a volcanic hill, and Charmes.

A good starting point is the *caveau* run by the Association des Producteurs du Cru Morgon (www.morgon.fr) in the cellars of the late-seventeenth-century château in the middle of the village, Chateau de Fontcrenne (Le Bourg, 69910 Villié-Morgon, tel: 04 74 04 20 99).

Distinguishing the *crus*: Morgon and Régnie

Gérard Méziat of the Domaine de la Combe aux Loups in Chiroubles also makes Regnié and Morgon. "Chiroubles is all about finesse, and about suppleness in the tannins. Of all the *crus*, it really is the most feminine – and aromatic. You find peonies, lily-of-the-valley, violets. Regnié has actually less tannin than Chiroubles, and is more about red fruit and redcurrants. Morgon is quite different: much more solid, more tannic, more spicy, more peppery-blackcurranty. We're at a high altitude here in Chiroubles, but very well exposed to the sun. But it's not that that makes the difference in the wine – it's the differences in the soil, the terroir."

Regnié-Durette: the youngest *cru*

This appellation, sandwiched between Morgon and Brouilly to the south, was promoted from Beaujolais-Villages in 1988 in response to appeals from the growers. It's symbolized by the church's two bell towers – clunky-looking nineteenth-century churches are as characteristic of Beaujolais as Romanesque ones are to the north. You can taste the characteristically juicy and supple wines in the Caveau des Deux Clochers (tel: 04 74

RIGHT *In the* cru *villages, Gamay is trained "en gobelel", without wires.*

FAR RIGHT *Vines are one of the few crops that can contend with the poor volcanic soils of northern Beaujolais.*

GROWERS IN BROUILLY, COTE DE BROUILLY, AND REGNIE

Jean-Claude Boisset
Le Pont des Samsons
69430 Quincié-en-Beaujolais
Tel: 04 74 69 09 30
(A/B4)
A big Burgundian négociant.

Alain Michaud
Beauvoir, 69220 St-Lager
Tel: 04 74 66 84 29 *(A3)*
Rich and long-lived Brouilly.

Domaine Joël Rochette
69430 Regnié-Durette
Tel: 04 74 35 78 *(B4)*
Quite rich wines, aged in big oak *foudres*, that even in this lightish appellation improve over two or three years.

Château Thivin
69460 Odenas
Tel: 04 74 03 47 53
(A3/4)
Claude Geoffray is one of the best growers in either appellation.

Domaine de la Voûte des Crozes
69220 Cercié
Tel: 04 74 66 85 29
(A/B3)
Look for lovely Côte de Brouilly.

PRICES: inexpensive

04 38 33, or look them up on the internet at www.vin-regnie.com).

Heading south

These four villages share the most southerly Beaujolais *cru* appellations, Brouilly and Côte de Brouilly. Both take their name from 300m (980-foot) high Mont-Brouilly. This hill, not sheer, but broad and commanding, is a plug of rock forced up through volcanic activity. Apart from the natural grandeur of this area, the Brouilly appellation is home to Beaujolais' (and Burgundy's) biggest wine estate, Château de la Chaize, based around a kind of mini-Versailles.

Take to your feet

Various footpaths lead up and around Mont-Brouilly, if you'd like to take a look at the area that way. From Odenas (A3/4) start at the town hall (*la mairie*) – from St-Lager (A3) start at the village *caveau*, Le Cuvage des Brouilly (tel: 04 74 66 82 65).

At the summit is the chapel of Nôtre Dame du Raisin (dedicated in 1857), the focus of a pilgrimage every September 8 to thank Our Lady for protecting the vines from mildew. From the summit well-marked footpaths lead around the hill as well as straight down.

Distinguishing the *crus*: Brouilly and Côtes de Brouilly

Claude Geoffray of Château Thivin makes Brouilly and Côte de Brouilly. What's the difference? "Brouilly is a much larger appellation than Côte de Brouilly: 1,260ha as opposed to 310ha. Brouilly is pink granite sands from the surrounding area; Côte de Brouilly is grey volcanic rock from the slopes of the hill itself, with a high copper content. You could say they were both feminine wines, but Côte de Brouilly is more aromatically subtle. There's a floral quality – violets, iris and peony – Brouilly is more simple red fruit."

In Odenas

The Château de la Chaize (69460 Odenas, tel: 04 74 03 41 05, www.chateaudelachaize.com), owns 94 ha of vines, and its cellars are built on an appropriately monumental scale. This property was built in 1676 to the designs of Jules Hardoin-Mansart (1646–1708) the architect of the Palace of Versailles, who gave his name to the mansard roof. The formal gardens were laid out by André Le Nôtre (1613–1700), who was responsible for Versaille's gardens (and also for reshaping St James' Park in London, formerly a deer park). The owner, the Marquise de Roussy de Sales, began a restoration programme in 1968. The wine is at the top of the range for a Brouilly, both in quality and price.

Château des Ravatys consists of a handsome nineteenth-century country house with vineyards. It was bequeathed to the Institut Pasteur in 1937 and since then the proceeds from its Côte de Brouilly have gone to fund medical research. (Château des Ravatys, Domaine de l'Institut Pasteur, 69220 St-Lager, tel: 04 74 66 80 35, www.chateaudesravatys.com)

Belleville

Belleville has an Olympic-size swimming pool, an eighteenth-century hospital, or "Hôtel-Dieu" with a ward like the one in Beaune, and a distant past within the frontiers of Muslim Europe: it was sacked by the eighth-century army of Emir Abd ur-Rahman, which Charles Martel, the grandfather of Charlemagne, later defeated at Tours. Stop here to experience old-fashioned Beaujolais at the négociant P. Ferraud et Fils (31 rue du maréchal Foch, 69220 Belleville-en-Beaujolais, tel: 04 74 06 47 60, www.ferraud.com). You can get more information at the Office de Tourisme (Hôtel Dieu, 68 rue de la

WHY BEAUJOLAIS IS LIKE NO OTHER FRENCH WINE

THE SOILS: in France, the country of argilo-calcaire ("chalky clay") soil, it's unusual to grow grapes on geologically ancient, acid, granitic soils like these.

THE GRAPE VARIETY: elsewhere Gamay was planted to make bulk wine in fairly northerly vineyards – not, as in Beaujolais, to be the main attraction.

THE CRUS: in the ten best villages, the crus, you only find bush vines, trained en gobelet (trained not on wires but as a bush). Mechanical harvesting can't be used.

THE WAY THE WINE'S MADE: whole bunches are piled in vats, without crushing. Enzymes start fermentation in the individual berries, and the vats fills with the carbon dioxide that results. It's called vinification beaujolaise or macération semi-carbonique, and produces wines with fresh, aromatic fruit characteristics.

WHERE TO EAT

ST-AMOUR:
Auberge du Paradis
Plâtre Durand
71570 St-Amour
Tel: 03 85 37 10 26
Mediterranean style.

Chez Jean-Pierre
Plâtre Durand
71570 St-Amour
Tel: 03 85 37 41 26

JULIENAS:
Le Coq
rue La Rabelette
69840 Juliénas
Tel: 04 74 04 41 98
A trendy take on the
"*bouchon* Lyonnais"
bistro-style.

CHENAS:
Les Platanes de Chénas
Les Deschamps
69840 Chénas
Tel: 03 85 36 79 80
Alsace-Beaujolais fusion.

ROMANECHE-THORINS:
Relais Beaujolais Bresse
La Maison Blanche
71570 Romanèche-Thorins
Tel: 03 85 35 51 93
Four-square Beaujolais
food.

FLEURIE:
Le Cep
place de l'Eglise
69820 Fleurie
Tel: 04 74 04 10 77
Top of the range.

CHIROUBLES:
La Terrasse du Beaujolais
route du Fût d'Avenas
69115 Chiroubles
Tel: 04 74 69 90 79

BROUILLY:
J.P. Croizier
Le Bourg
69220 St-Lager
Tel: 04 74 66 82 79
An ideal lunch place.

République 69823 Belleville, Tel: 04 74 66 44 67).

St-Jean-d'Ardières
On the RN6, the main road to Lyon and the South, is the Maison des Beaujolais (tel: 04 74 66 16 46), with restaurant, shop, and tasting area. It is focused exclusively on the home region, with no wines on show from anywhere else.

Where to stay
Try a rebuilt twelfth-century château, occupied at various times by the Nanton and Pizay families, the Wehrmacht, and a négociant. Now it's a luxury hotel. It's called Chateau de Pizay, and it's at 69220 St-Jean-d'Ardières (tel: 04 74 66 26 10). Even if you don't go to stay, perhaps eat here and taste the estate's organic wine, and admire the sculptural symmetry of another of Le Nôtre's seventeenth-century gardens. I especially liked winemaker Pascal Dufaitre's Beaujolais Blanc.

Other options: St-Amour, Juliénas, Chiroubles
In St-Amour, there's Le Paradis de Marie Les Ravinets (71570 St Amour, tel: 03 85 36 51 90). It's not expensive. In Juliénas, try Chez La Rose (rue La Rabelette, 69840 Juliénas, tel: 04 74 04 41 20) and, in Chiroubles, Alain et Véronique Passot, Domaine de la Grosse Pierre (69115 Chiroubles, tel: 04 74 69 12 17). The last-named does *chambres d'hôte*.

And in Romanèche-Thorins, Villié-Morgon, and Brouilly
If you want to stay in Romanèche-Thorins try Les Maritonnes, (71570 Romanèche Thorins, tel: 03 85 35 51 70). This is an upmarket place handy for the Duboeuf experience.

In Villié-Morgon Jean Foillard has some groovily-decorated *chambres d'hôte*, recommended by visiting wine writers (Le Clachet, 69910 Villié-Morgon, tel : 04 74 04 24 97).

Brouilly has the Hôtel-Restaurant du Mont Brouilly, at Le Pont des Samsons (69430 Quincié, tel: 04 74 04 33 73).

Or if you fancy camping, there's a campsite at La Verne, (69820 Fleurie, tel: 04 74 69 80 07).

Beaujolais Villages and Terres des Pierres Dorées

B eaujolais Villages is a catch-all appellation: in 1950 it replaced the old, unwieldy system in which, rather like the Mâconnais, scores of villages had the right to tack their name on to that of Beaujolais. But that doesn't mean that Beaujolais Villages is a homogeneous appellation: in fact non-*cru* Beaujolais is so diverse that in this last chapter I'm going to suggest three separate routes.

Our first route is one for the Beaujolais Villages and plain Beaujolais communities that encircle the *cru* villages. The second is one for the other patch of Beaujolais Villages south of Mont Brouilly, immortalized by Gabriel Chevallier's novel Clochemerle. Thirdly we travel to the Bas Beaujolais, or Terres des Pierres Dorées, an area attached to Lyon that in the early middle ages was separate from, and at times at war with, the upper Beaujolais ruled by the lords or "Sires" of Beaujeu, the ancient capital.

Route one: shadowing the cru (*see* map p.133)
We start by shadowing the *cru* villages visited in the last chapter, and in some cases retracing the route already taken. The places we're seeing now didn't make it to *cru* status because they're too mountainous (this is the case with the first part of the circuit that runs from Jullié to Beaujeu, via Emeringes and Vauxrenard) or because they're too far down in the sandy soils of the plain (Corcelles and Lancié). We travel between these two groups of villages along the region's axis, the valley of the Ardières, that links Beaujeu and Belleville.

Above their league
Some of Beaujolais' most important growers are based in non-*cru* villages. Growers such as Jean-Paul Dubost in Lantignié (*D2*) or Pierre Gelin's Domaine des Nugues and André Collonge, both in Lancié (*E1/2*) belong in Beaujolais' premier league.

Jullié
Jullié's Fête du Vin Nouveau is in October, though the wine goes on sale, as elsewhere, on the third Thursday in November. Walk up to the little twelfth-century Chapelle de Vâtre for some breathtaking views. There's

LEFT *Vine prunings make excellent wood for barbeques.*

BELOW *Golden slumbers: the sleepy south of Beaujolais really does glow in the sun.*

**GROWERS ON ROUTE ONE
(IN ORDER OF ROUTE)**
. . . .

Domaine de Monsepeys
Les Benons
69840 Emeringes
Tel: 04 74 04 45 11 *(E2)*
http://perso.wanadoo.fr/
domaine.de.monsepeys/
Minimal use of fertilisers,
and low yields.

Domaine de Gry-Sablon
Les Chavannes
69840 Emeringes
Tel: 04 74 04 45 35 *(E2)*
Non-*cru* Emeringes as well
as Fleurie and Morgon.

Domaine de l'Oisillon
Bourg, 69820 Vauxrenard
Tel: 04 74 69 90 51 *(E3)*

Domaine J. et S. Dory
Bourg, 69820 Vauxrenard
Tel: 04 74 69 91 89 *(E3)*
Award-winning domaine.

Philippe Deschamps
Morne, 69430 Beaujeu
Tel: 04 74 04 82 54 *(D2)*
Gets good critical attention.

**Henri Dubost et Fils
Domaine du Tracot**
69430 Lantignié
Tel: 04 74 04 87 51 *(D2)*
Very good. Also *chambres
d'hôte.*

**Gilles Perroud
Château du Basty**
69430 Lantignié
Tel: 04 74 04 85 98 *(D2)*
Nice lightish Villages.

Domaine C. et M. Joubert
Le Bourg, 69430 Lantignié
Tel: 04 74 04 81 37 *(D2)*
Crus and serious Villages.

Domaine de la Sorbière
La Roche, 69430
Quincié-en-Beaujolais
Tel: 04 74 69 06 82 *(D2)*
Interesting wines.

PRICES: inexpensive

a village *caveau de dégustation*. Georgette and Thierry Descombes (Les Vignes, 69840 Jullié, tel: 04 74 04 42 03) make Juliénas, but also a *cuvee vielles vignes* from the Quatres Cerisiers vineyard – both are very good. Another local grower, Robert Bridet of the Domaine de la Roche Mère (207 Le Bourg, 69840 Jullié, tel: 04 74 04 42 32) is one of the best producers of Moulin-à-Vent. Also recommended is Jérome Corsin, (Les Vignes, 69840 Jullié, tel: 06 81 27 31 55).

Emeringes and Vauxrenard
Neither Emeringes' Château du Chaylard nor its Le Nôtre gardens (*see* p.129) are open for visits, but it's worth coming here to eat at the popular Auberge des Vignerons (*see* box, p.137).

Vauxrenard is surrounded by vine-covered hills, and dominated by the chunky eleventh-century Romanesque tower of the church of St Martin. There's a 2.8km (1.7-mile) vineyard walk, which takes place from April to the end of August and is led by a local winemaker.

Beaujeu – the old capital
This town gave the Beaujolais region its name and was its capital until 1514. In the early middle ages, the Sires de Beaujeu from the now-ruined Château de Pierre Aiguë, just outside the town, controlled the strategically important valley of the Ardières which links the Rhône Valley and the south with the Loire and the north.

A wine museum called Les Sources du Beaujolais has themed displays on the region's history, geography, and legends. A three-in-one ticket also gets you into the local history/folklore museum of Marius Audin, with its collection of wax fashion models, and into the *caveau* ("Le Temple de Bacchus") in the basement of the town hall.

Condiment tourism: not mustard this time but top-of-the-range nut oils (walnut, hazelnut, almond, and so on) from the Huilerie Beaujolaise (29 rue des Écharmeaux, 69430 Beaujeu, tel: 04 74 69 28 06).

Beaujolais' Voie Verte – a former branch line turned cycle route runs down the valley of the Ardières to St-Jean-d'Ardières. Bikes for hire can be delivered from Avenas for a minimum of ten people, from the bar/general store there, La Table Ronde (tel: 04 74 69 97 61).

Quincié-en-Beaujolais and Cercié
Cercié is vulgarly known as "Pisse Vieille" ("Piss, old woman"), a name that appears on some producers' labels, from the legend of an old village woman who mistook her confessor's admonition, *"ne pechez plus"* ("sin no more") for *"ne pissez plus"* and tried to obey, with uncomfortable consequences.

From Belleville to St-Jean-Ardières you are on Route Nationale 6, the former Roman road and the old "Route du Soleil" to Lyon. St-Jean itself is on sandy soils that qualify only for the basic Beaujolais appellation, but one local producer makes the most of this somewhat unpromising terroir, Georges Barjot at Domaine de Jasseron (Grille-Midi, 69220 St-Jean-d'Ardières, tel: 04 74 66 47 34).

The fifteenth-century château at Corcelles-en-Beaujolais (tel: 04 74 66 00 24), is also a big producer that is a regular winner of awards for

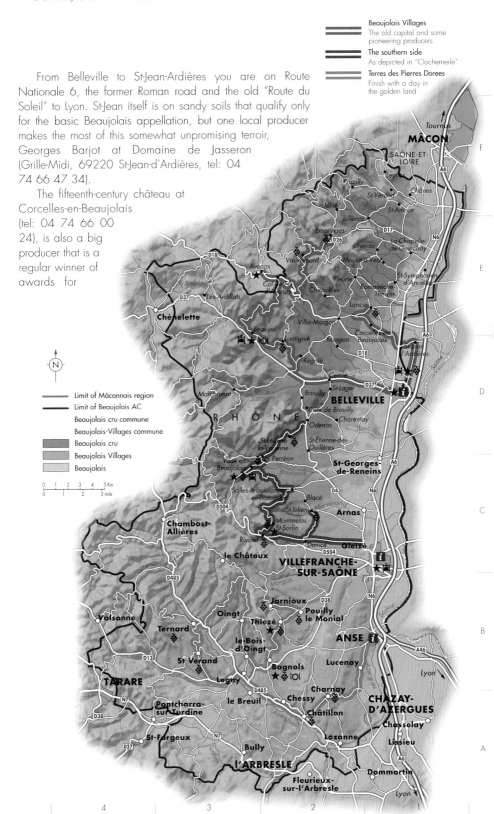

Beaujolais Villages
The old capital and some pioneering producers

The southern side
As depicted in "Clochemerle"

Terres des Pierres Dorees
Finish with a day in the golden land

N

Limit of Mâconnais region
Limit of Beaujolais AC
Beaujolais *cru* commune
Beaujolais-Villages commune
Beaujolais *cru*
Beaujolais Villages
Beaujolais

0 1 2 3 4 5 Km
0 1 2 3 mile

ABOVE *In Beaujeu, the town that gave Beaujolais its name.*

RIGHT *In Vaux, the pissoir that made the author Gabriel Chevallier's fortune.*

its quite commercial Beaujolais Villages made from widely separated vineyards.

Lancié nearby *(E2)* is home to Pierre Gelin's Domaine des Nugues (Les Pasquiers, 69220 Lancié, tel: 04 74 04 14 00), which makes the kind of lowish-acidity wine you might (rightly) expect to appeal to ultra-powerful American wine critic Robert Parker – good stuff that actually reminds me a little of a Rhône Grenache.

André Colonge (Les Terres Dessus, 69220 Lancié, tel: 04 74 04 11 73) is also very good – he makes a lighter, rather mineral, delicious wine; if this sounds like your kind of thing, Sylvain Rosier at the Château du Châtelard (69220 Lancié, tel: 04 74 04 12 99) makes wines with the same emphasis on freshness.

Route two: the southern parts

Here we start south of Mont Brouilly, the southernmost *cru*, and wind towards Villefranche-sur-Saône via Vaux-en-Beaujolais, the fictional Clochemerle of Gabriel Chevallier (1895–1969), Salles-Arbuissonnas, and Montmelas.

Chevallier's 1934 novel, *Clochemerle*, is an affectionate satire of rural life, based on the entrenched conflict between the church and local nobility, and the anti-clerical Left, symbolized by a socialist mayor who provokes the local clergy by building a urinal outside the church.

Guy Jacquemont, responsible for Château de Ravatys and the Domaine de la Rochelle (*see* p.129 and 124), likens the book's vast success to Peter Mayle's *Year in Provence*: "At that time, industry had already started to draw on the countryside to provide its labour force, and the book's readers enjoyed revisiting their roots."

There are important growers in each of Beaujolais' St-Etiennes: in St-Etienne-des-Oullières, Château de Lacarelle (69460 St-Etienne-des-Oullières, tel: 04 74 03 40 80) makes very good fresh and balanced Beaujolais Villages on a very large scale; it has 140ha of vines. Just 3km (2 miles) away in the twin village of St-Étienne-la-Varenne you can find Jean-Claude Lapalu (Le Petit Vernay, 69460 St-Etienne-la-Varenne,

LOCAL INFORMATION

Office de Tourisme
Place de l'Hôtel de Ville
69430 Beaujeu
Tel: 04 74 69 22 88
www.beaujeu.com

Villefranche-sur-Saône
96 rue de la Sous-
Préfecture, 69400 Beaujeu
Tel: 04 74 07 27 40

Anse
place du 8 Mai
Beaujeu 69480
Tel: 04 74 60 26 16

tel: 04 74 03 50 57), a non-certified but largely organic grower who puts more emphasis on concentration.

Le Perréon
Here you can meet a leading advocate of making Beaujolais as if it were burgundy – destemming the grapes and crushing them instead of using the traditional Beaujolais method of fermenting whole bunches with their stems. Bruno Bérerd (Domaine de la Madone, Le Bourg, 69460 Le Perreon, tel: 04 74 03 21 85) then matures his best wines in barrel.

"We've been doing it for eight or nine years," he says. "I wouldn't say it's approved by the authorities – we're tolerated." They're good wines, though personally I'd welcome a little more (unfashionable) acidity.

Vaux-en-Beaujolais
There is now a Musée de la Vigne et du Vin and a tasting cellar (tel: 04 74 03 26 58) here – and one Georges Dufour runs a private tasting cellar in very Clochemerle-like competition with it (tel: 04 74 03 23 60). Anne Mathon, formerly head of publicity for Beaujolais' Bureau Interprofessionel, is a local grower (tel: 06 86 77 07 79). Vaux is living up to its official status as one of the region's "Oenological Centres of Interest".

Salles-Arbuissonnas
The monks of Cluny founded a priory here. There are fifteenth-century frescos, though nothing to rival Berzé-la-Ville (see p.118), and a beautiful and tranquil Romanesque cloister. Salles has a small museum of viticulture, and an enterprizing

GROWERS ON ROUTE TWO

Domaine de la Chaumière Montrichard
69460 Vaux-en-Beaujolais
Tel: 04 74 02 15 11 *(C3)*
A good rosé and deep red wines, made with *grillage* (a grille keeps the grapes and stems immersed in the fermenting wine).

Domaine de la Combe des Fées
La Maison Jaune
69460 Vaux-en-Beaujolais
Tel: 04 74 03 24 55 *(C3)*
Elegant, not powerful wines.

Château de Vaux
Marie-Ange de Vermont
Le Bourg
69460 Vaux-en-Beaujolais
Tel: 04 74 03 23 65 *(C3)*
Juicy, well-balanced Villages.

PRICES: inexpensive

GROWERS ON ROUTE THREE

Château de Boisfranc
Thierry Doat
69640 Jarnioux
04 74 68 88 88 *(B2/3)*
Organic since 1982. There
are a couple of *chambres
d'hôte* here.

Domaine de Baluce
Le Plan
69620 Bagnols
Tel: 04 74 41 71 43 *(B2)*
White Beaujolais as well.
Original and full wines
from a grower who's open
to experimentation.

Domaine du Milhomme
69620 Ternand
Tel: 04 74 71 33 13 *(B3)*
Full-bodied wine.

Domaine du Vissoux
69260 St-Vérand
Tel: 04 74 71 79 42 *(B3)*
See main text.

Jean-Gilles Chasselay
La Roche
69820 Châtillon
d'Azergues
Tel: 04 78 47 93 73 *(A2)*
Jean-Gilles and his wife
are as good as explaining
wine as at making it.

Jean-Paul Brun
Les Crières
69380 Charnay
Tel: 04 78 47 93 45 *(A2)*
See main text.

Domaine du Moulin Blanc
Les Crières
69380 Charnay
Tel: 04 78 43 98 60 *(A2)*
Excellent red and white.

Clos des Vieux
Marronniers
69380 Charnay
Tel: 04 78 47 95 28 *(A2)*
Minimal chemical use.

PRICES: inexpensive

grower who's recently created a *caveau* and a *gîte* at his family estate. This is Domaine Christian Miolane (La Folie, 69460 Salles-Arbuissonas, tel: 04 74 67 52 67).

Montmelas-St-Sorlin

Like many châteaux that look too good to be true, the Château de Montmelas is just that – it's a collaboration between its fourteenth-century builders and the ubiquitous gothic revivalist Viollet-le-Duc (1814–79). It's also a successful producer of Beaujolais Villages. Visits (normally groups only) can be arranged by appointment (tel: 04 74 67 32 94).

Beside the château, but with a postal address in neighbouring Denicé, is a grower worth visiting: he's Frédéric Sambardier, and the estate is Domaine Manoir du Carra (69640 Denicé, tel: 04 74 67 38 04). He makes concentrated, spicy, unfiltered wines.

Villefranche-sur-Saône – the new capital

Beaujolais' capital is a handsome town on the Saône built around a core of Renaissance streets. Don't miss the market, every morning in front of the town hall – it is great for local cheeses, charcuterie, honey….

There's a wine school offering tasting courses that can be combined with vineyard visits on foot or by bicycle, and even with golfing. Ecole Beaujolaise des Vin (Inter Beaujolais, Nathalie Aoulay, 210 boulevard Vermorel, 69661 Villefranche, tel: 04 74 02 22 18).

On the left bank of the Saône, 7km (4 miles) from Villefranche on the D933, is an extraordinary architectural masterpiece from the same period as Cormatin in the Mâconnais, but on a vaster scale: the Château de Fléchères (01480 Fareins, tel: 04 74 67 86 59).

Route three: the Terres des Pierres Dorées

If Beaujolais is a low-status wine, in this area, which largely lives from selling Beaujolais Nouveau, you might expect to be scraping the barrel. The reality is that this is a lovely region which looks quite different to the granite hills to the north, and is home to several of the region's big guns.

This itinerary descends in a clockwise loop from Villefranche: it goes to Pouilly-le-Monial, Jarnioux, the hill village of Theizé, Bagnols, Oignt, Ternand, and Charnay, and ends in Anse, just south of Villefranche.

Almost every village has kept some medieval fortifications. In the early thirteenth century, this region was on the front line in a war between the Sires de Beaujeu, allied to the French monarchy, and the local ruler, the Archbishop of Lyon. Villefranche, a Beaujeu possession, confronted Anse, the Lyon front line. There is a legacy of stunning military architecture in Bagnols, Oingt and Ternand, and in Anse itself with the striking Château de Tours.

Golden stones

Calling the part of Beaujolais that makes the cheapest wine the Pays des Pierres Dorées sounds like rebranding, until you see the villages, churches, and castles: a dream of the golden South, as shot by an especially self-indulgent lighting director.

Why does the limestone glow? Crushed shells give it its texture, and iron oxide its colour. It's the right geology not for great Gamay wines but for Pinot and Chardonnay, as Jean-Paul Brun (see below) has observed. There were quarries at Jarnioux, Theizé and Bagnols.

High profile in the Bas Beaujolais

The biggest name has for years been Jean-Paul Brun, based in Charnay (not to be confused with Charnay-lès-Mâcon, 55km/34 miles north up the A6 motorway). Brun has for years rejected the technological aids used by his colleagues and claimed to work *à la ancienne*, using Burgundian techniques, growing Pinot Noir and achieving price levels and overseas sales that his neighbours could only dream of. Brun now also works as a négociant in several *cru* appellations.

Pierre Chermette in St-Vérand (another name that appears in north and south) is another non-conformist: a critic of Beaujolais' reliance on chaptalization. His success has enabled him to buy into the *crus*, and his Domaine du Vissoux is now also a producer of Moulin-à-Vent and Fleurie.

Finally, (but first in this route) is one of Beaujolais' fully certified organic producers: Thierry Doat of the Château de Boisfranc. None of these three growers, incidentally, are too grand to make Beaujolais Nouveau.

ABOVE *Bring back the empties: local growers often make basic wine for their neighbours*

LEFT *Last year's vine tendrils, still on the wire.*

WHERE TO EAT

Auberge des Vignerons
69840 Emeringes
Tel: 04 74 04 45 72
Very popular, so book.

Buffet de la Gare
La Gare, 69220 Belleville
Tel: 04 74 66 07 36
Not a normal station buffet – more like the one of your dreams.

Restaurant Le Cèdre
196 rue de Roncevaux
69400 Villefranche
Tel: 04 74 62 95 91
Pig's trotters and so on.

Restaurant Le Faisan Doré
686 route de Beauregard
69400 Villefranche
Tel: 04 74 65 01 66
Ambitious, on the Saône.

Château de Bagnols
69620 Bagnols
Tel: 04 74 71 40 00
Hotel-restaurant in a medieval castle. Nicole Kidman and Tom Cruise stayed here.

Domaine du Moulin Blanc
69380 Charnay
See p.136.

RIGHT *Throughout Burgundy, but especially in Beaujolais, wine growers often boost their income by renting out a gîte.*

WHERE TO STAY

JULLIE: **Les Chanoriers**
Tel 04 74 04 46 12
A small campsite.

EMERINGES:
Domaine de Monsepeys
Chambres d'hôte
(see p.132).

BEAUJEU: **Anne de Beaujeu**
28 rue de la République
69430 Beaujeu
Tel: 04 74 04 88 61
Fairly upmarket. Also an
ambitious restaurant.

LANTIGNIE: **Jean-Paul Dubost**
See p.132.

VAUX-EN-BEAUJOLAIS:
Auberge de Clochemerle
rue Gabriel Chevallier
69460 Vaux-en-Beaujolais
Tel: 04 74 03 20 16
Traditional values.

VILLEFRANCHE:
**Hotel Restaurant La Ferme
du Poulet**
180 rue George Mangin
69400 Villefranche
Tel: 04 74 62 19 07
Out of the way and in
an industrial area, but
this old posthouse is
worth discovering.

BAGNOLS:
Château de Bagnols
69620 Bagnols
Tel: 04 74 71 40 00
See p.137.

Time off from wine

At Pouilly-le-Monial, stop at the village church to see the sixteenth-century stained glass window of the Flight into Egypt. Jarnioux's castle dates from the thirteenth century – the six towers are renaissance additions. In Theizé it's worth stopping at the top of the village just for the view. The nearby Château de Rochebonne (tel: 04 74 71 16 10) has exhibitions about the region and its winemaking traditions; its former chapel has late gothic additions to its original Romanesque structure. It's now used for concerts and temporary exhibitions.

In Bagnols, instead of visiting a castle you can stay in one: the fifteenth-century château is a luxury hotel and restaurant. Make sure your room is at least as good as the one occupied by Nicole Kidman and Tom Cruise.

Oingt and Ternand (*B3*) are both fabulous medieval hill villages. Oingt has grown around the remains of a thirteenth-century castle, whose chapel is now the village church and whose keep, or *donjon*, is the local landmark. Ternand – a former possession of the archbishops of Lyon – is also fortified. Look especially for the eighth-century wall paintings in the crypt of the village church. Charnay's village square is a harmonious ensemble of late medieval houses in golden limestone. In St-Jean-des-Vignes, there's a geological museum, Espace Pierres Folles.

After all this wine tourism you may worry about becoming train-spotter-ish. So reassure yourself by meeting the real thing – the enthusiasts who run the miniature railway in the capital of the Terres des Pierres Dorées, Anse, whose 2.5km (1.5-mile) miniature railway is faithfully modelled on real SNCF rolling stock. Track them down at the Association de la Voie de 38cm (8 avenue de la Libération, 69480 Anse, tel: 04 74 60 26 01 www.trains-fr.org/unecto/anse).

Bibliography and further reading

Bibliography
In addition to the further reading listed below:

Michel Bettane and Thierry Dessauve, *Classement des Meilleurs Vins de France*, Editions de la Revue de Vin de France, Paris, 2003.

Jean-Pierre Coffe and Thomas Bravo-Maza, *Mes Vins Preferés à Moins de E10*, Plon, Paris, 2003.

Antoine Gerbelle and Philippe Maurange, *Le Guide des Meilleurs Vins à Petits Prix*, Editions de la Revue de Vin de France, Paris, 2003.

Jacques Néauport (ed.), *Jules Chauvet ou le Talent du Vin*, Jean-Paul Roche, Paris, 1997.

Jacky Rigaux and Christian Bon, *Les Nouveaux Vignerons*, Le Reveil des Terroirs, Editions de Bourgogne, Dijon, 2003.

Further reading
To complete the Burgundy experience, some classic works:

Serena Sutcliffe MW, *The Wines of Burgundy*, Mitchell Beazley, London, 2003.

Matt Kramer, *Making Sense of Burgundy*, William Morrow (currently out of print).

Anthony Hanson MW, *Classic Wine Library Burgundy*, Mitchell Beazley, London, 1999 (reprinted under new title in 2003).

Clive Coates MW, *Côte d'Or*, Weidenfeld and Nicholson, London, 1997 – a magisterial work.

Le Guide Hachette des Vins, Hachette Livre, Paris, 2003.

Austen Biss and Owen Smith, *The Wines of Chablis*, Writers International Ltd Bournemouth, 2000.

And if the bug really bites, you'll want to subscribe to:
Allen Meadows, *Burghound* – a definitive, if pricey, quarterly newsletter, details on burghound.com